College Dropout

Creating Your Passive Income
Laptop Lifestyle

*(How a College Dropout Makes $50,000 a Month
While Traveling the World)*

Michael Fortune

Published By **Tyson Maxwell**

Michael Fortune

All Rights Reserved

College Dropout: Creating Your Passive Income Laptop Lifestyle (How a College Dropout Makes $50,000 a Month While Traveling the World)

ISBN 978-1-7771462-5-2

No part of this guidebook shall be reproduced in any form without permission in writing from the publisher except in the case of brief quotations embodied in critical articles or reviews.

Legal & Disclaimer

The information contained in this book is not designed to replace or take the place of any form of medicine or professional medical advice. The information in this book has been provided for educational & entertainment purposes only.

The information contained in this book has been compiled from sources deemed reliable, and it is accurate to the best of the Author's knowledge; however, the Author cannot guarantee its accuracy and validity and cannot be held liable for any errors or omissions. Changes are periodically made to this book. You must consult your doctor or get professional medical advice before using any of the suggested remedies, techniques, or information in this book.

Upon using the information contained in this book, you agree to hold harmless the Author from and against any damages, costs, and expenses, including any legal fees potentially resulting from the application of any of the information provided by this guide. This disclaimer applies to any damages or injury caused by the use and application, whether directly or indirectly, of any advice or information presented, whether for breach of contract, tort, negligence, personal injury, criminal intent, or under any other cause of action.

You agree to accept all risks of using the information presented inside this book. You need to consult a professional medical practitioner in order to ensure you are both able and healthy enough to participate in this program.

Table Of Contents

Chapter 1: The Billionaire Mindset and How to develop it 1

Chapter 2: A College Degree Will Not You A Billionaire 17

Chapter 3: The Dropout Mindset 36

Chapter 4: Billionaires Who Left College before Graduating 46

Chapter 5: Ten Traits of Billionaires That Make Them Successful 65

Chapter 6: How to Have a Billionaire Mindset: Tips for Becoming A Rich, Successful Person................................... 96

Chapter 7: leaving College with success 105

Chapter 8: They Made Them Highly Skilled 124

Chapter 9: the read Many Books on Numerous Topics 134

Chapter 10: They Started While Studying and Then Dropped Out 144

Chapter 11: They Had a Dear Path Of Future 154

Chapter 12: They Were Working For Very Long Hours, Even For Nothing 172

Chapter 1: The Billionaire Mindset and How to develop it

The mindset of a billionaire is committed to success, and is defined by determination and concentration. It is also marked by originality, creativity as well as tolerance and compassion. Although everyone wants to become billionaires but what proportion of us have what it takes to be successful? A tiny portion of the 8 billion residents can be said that they are billionaires. They're the people who've created extremely profitable companies and have contributed greatly to the advancement of mankind.

Millionaires, contrary to what many believe, are not simply wealthy. How they view prosperity and wealth is distinct for the billionaires. Security in the financial realm isn't an additional priority for them. Instead, it's an asset for making cash and opening doors. They do not think there's a perpetual shortage of money however, they believe it can be accumulated and invested. The trick to success, as exemplified by billionaires around the globe is to consider the bigger picture and look at the longer-term perspective of any endeavor they choose to pursue. It's not all about secure financial stability. The value and wealth should be created in order to sustain over time.

What is the reason you think they owe to their success? What is the question, then, how do you achieve the mind-set of billionaires? This is a few examples of thoughts that might be circulating through your head. There are commonalities in billionaires who help them achieve their goals. You can also learn to nurture these characteristics and witness your life turning around throughout the years.

Life's dynamic perspective is the biggest asset of billionaires.

In the course of your daily the world and face new circumstances you should rely on the skills you've learned rather than your natural ones. There are also other shifts regarding your perspective that you'll need to undergo if you wish to become a millionaire. In order to be a billionaire, you must not just think about yourself as the of a billionaire. You must also carry yourself in the same manner.

Strategies for Thinking Like a Billionaire

The idea that wealth has a decisive impact is the first step towards becoming a billionaire. Eliminating that illusion will help you to work towards your goals in the right direction. It is not a good idea to view money as an end all in it's own right, but instead as a way to achieve get to the end. The brains of billionaires tend to be occupied by big plans and a glance towards the future.

They are realistic regarding what they will need to be successful and are ready to invest the energy and the time required to achieve their goals. Additionally, they're not scared to plunge into the water in the event of a difficult scenario. In addition, billionaires are able to have optimism and believe in their ability. One of the first steps to achieving the success level attained by billionaires is to adopt their mind frame and other behaviors. Here are six strategies to make you think as billionaires.

Time is money and wealth is health.

In the process of building fortune, billionaires are aware the importance of starting their day early. They rise before dawn and make use of cooks, chauffeurs as well as personal butlers and other people, in order to have some time for their targets and wellbeing. If it comes to their wellbeing and the environment their environment, they place both on the top of their list.

A healthy body is vital to reaching your goals. You must control your temper because in the best wisdom of Vipassana meditation show, anger creates a tiny amount of poison to get dispersed to all of the cells in your body.

If your mental well-being is healthy then you'll be able perform at your best that will do wonders to boost your self-confidence.

Millionaires see time in a different way. They have a meticulous plan and make the most of their time as they recognize its importance. They're not shy about delegating responsibilities to others to allow them to focus on their goal. They're aware of the need to spend their energy and time for success. Alongside living today and making plans for what's to come in the near future for their career as well as their personal lives. They are meticulous in the way they set goals and show incredible patience when working towards their objectives. All of it adds up to the fact that billionaires are adept in making the most out of their time.

The billionaires of the world are of the opinion that early rising is crucial to their achievement. The majority of respondents said they get up before 5:15 each day.

An unadulterated, raw energy is felt throughout the early morning, when the sun's huge orange sky is only beginning to increase. It is a time to think clearly and get your work done and begin preparing for the day using the additional time available. It's great to start your day when most sleep.

Remember that reducing your sleeping hours won't increase your productivity. A few billionaires are able to survive with just 4 to 5 hours sleep, while the majority of people are able to are happiest with at least seven. People who require more sleep are able to get their Zs earlier.

Develop discipline

This is also true for both your personal and professional lives and you'll fail in the event that you do not have control to apply your strategies regularly. Remove as many obstacles that hinder your progress as you are able to. Reach your goal quickly. Imagine yourself as someone who's always striving to be better.

The common belief is that billionaires possess special skills. They're just as the rest of us. Sometimes, they have a lack of motivation and drive. However, they are aware of that fact and are determined not to allow this to cause the state of apathy. They continue to fight regardless of the circumstances.

Make an investment in a mentor coach

Each of these hundreds billionaires have a coach who has helped them reach the very top. A coach is someone who will keep you constantly on the right track. Coaches also aid in self-analysis and maximise your abilities. The most crucial element of the game is your own mental state, which is why they make investments accordingly.

Establish patterns

If performed regularly, routines and rituals can bring significant and long-lasting results. There is a common belief that in the morning, most billionaires begin their days.

While the routines of the billionaires in the world vary from simple to complicated exercise, making time for study, and pondering are commonplace activities.

Be bold and deliberate.

A billionaire no matter how bad circumstances get, makes a decision to risk it all and conquers their fears and strives to be the best at every aspect of their life, including sending emails, to facilitating meetings.

Continuously seeking ways to grow will help you improve your self-esteem. It's not a matter of luck in having a head start over one percent of the population and so they'll develop a strategy and follow it through. It is important to have long-term goals However, the right books demonstrate that a majority of those who are wealthy are also focused on the present and today.

What You Should Know!

Do you think of yourself with the title of billionaire? Do you have the middle class approach to thinking? The wealthy have a style of thinking that the vast majority aren't aware of. The common belief is that rich people are only concerned in increasing their fortune. It's not always the case but. They are able to perform more work in their free time is an important draw for the majority of their peers. They also are smitten with passion for their earning a living. This is an ideal scenario to be in. If you're fed up of having to scrape out of paycheque to paycheck and you're fed up of being unable to afford the money needed to follow your dreams now is the perfect time to adopt the mindset of a millionaire and establish your own compass toward achieving greatness.

The same fundamental steps billionaires such as Bill Gates, Elon Musk as well as Jeff Bezos have used to achieve success.

If you want to be a millionaire The first step is determine what you'd like to have and work towards it. Many people, unfortunately, don't want to make the commitment needed to accomplish their goals. While they're capable, they trick themselves into believing that they're incompetent. The ability to overcome challenges through creative thinking is the strength of millions of billionaires around the globe and is a major factor in their achievement. It demonstrates your commitment to the subject, and could enhance your problem-solving skills. The will to go to the source of your desires, and to achieve them, requires not taking advantage of others, instead, but gaining what you want to achieve without resorting in dishonest ways.

The other requirement of an attitude of a billionaire is the ability to make investments instead of throwing away money. If it's about spending billionaires tend to be extremely thrifty due to their experience in learning the approach to saving and investing that will bring the best yields. The billionaires eventually leave the job they're working at and become the boss of their own. The trick is to shift the perspective of your life and allow your money do the job on your behalf, not doing it for you. Instead of investing more than 1000 dollars for the most recent iPhone it is possible for that money to be wisely invested and most likely triple or double in value over the next few years. Even though you gave your iPhone but everyone is aware that this tradeoff was justifiable, considering the sum of money you got in return.

The next step is to envision enormous success for yourself realizing that nothing is beyond reach as that you push your limits. Although it's true that it's best to start at a low level however that doesn't mean that you shouldn't be able to dream; the chance of achieving your goal could be sooner than anticipated. Don't be afraid of having to fail at completing a huge job. In fact the failure could present the opportunity to understand your mistakes. Even if, in the beginning you fail but you'll be able to be able to enjoy the stars.

There's a time at which you're determined to continue studying, however it's not uncommon for people to not make time for learning after they have completed formal schooling. Successful people maintain their minds open and are able to retain information. Warren Buffet, who is valued at $109.5 billion as at the time of writing, stated that he had read more than a hundred investment-related books before the time he turned 20. When you graduate from college, the majority of people don't read any more books. Also, it's important to increase your knowledge and experience. Learn as much as you can about the topic in case you're fascinated. It's surprising how often irrelevant skills can prove useful in unexpected ways.

Finally, set yourself a challenge by setting high goals. Nobody has accomplished something without setting out precise goals. Anyone who boasts that you can make money quickly is deceiving themselves. Beware of pursuing wealth for quick in any way. Aims that are unrealistic can only make you feel dissatisfied and depressed. One example is to you set the goal of the accumulation of one million dollars worth of wealth in the first few years of your life as an initial goal. Do not spend your money in frills. Instead, place it towards your future, and propel your self to greater heights. So, you'll be able to ensure that you'll not be short of funds to achieve your goals.

People who have accumulated billions and millions of dollars are able to have a completely different attitude than the typical Joe. They're naive and adventurous without worrying about the smallest aspects or hesitation to attempt something new. They have an "whatever it requires" approach that is constantly looking for the next challenge and opportunities for growth. The way they think propels the team to unimaginable levels and fills their lives with happiness and joy. They're not stifled by fear or doubt and are ready to tackle the new challenges. The best way to approach this is to adopt that mindset and attitude as a millionaire If you want to achieve greater things in your the world.

In summary, set your sights high and put in the work required to reach your goals Avoid unnecessary spending through smart investment decisions. You might have the skills to be one day Bill Gates.

Chapter 2: A College Degree Will Not You A Billionaire

As the times have changed, the need to earn a college degree has become the same as it was. The school curriculum was thought as the essential ingredient to the success and wealth. In order to manage businesses and complete transactions, one must possess an education that is of the highest quality. However, due to the way things have changed in the last few years that a degree from a university does not guarantee of prosperity in the future.

The billionaire real property developer Donald Trump famously remarked that an education in college alone will not prepare students to live their lives following the graduation. You won't be able to achieve success and be successful when you only apply your knowledge acquired during your time at school, as you don't get the required experiences in real life.

More than that the requirement of a college degree, it is required to excel at work and in your job. For success in your career it is necessary to possess many skills that include management, negotiation, great attitudes, positive thinking and business acumen. They won't teach these requirements in the classroom.

According to billionaire Elon Musk, who co-founded SpaceX as well as Tesla the traditional method of educational and learning at schools can be compared to getting data in your brain, which can be problematic because it is impossible to know whether the data you collect can be useful to you.

Not Everyone Fits Into the Ideal Education System

Seth Godin, a marketing consultant and best-selling author, declared in a talk that our education system is prone to have more followers than for those who lead. The schools train students to be followers that accept tasks and perform the tasks. Also, it is necessary become an instrument and limit and limit your initial thought.

Furthermore, our society and most schools force students to be focused in achieving the highest grades in their tests than studying everything they can in classes. The most famous quote from the brilliant creator Thomas Edison goes as follows: "Tomorrow is my test, but I don't care because a single sheet of paper can't decide my destiny."

A formal education and graduation from a college degree could aid you to achieve your objective of joining the company as a highly skilled white-collar employee. That's the only thing you need to know. But, the vast majority of people prefer an occupation and business instead of a job.

For that, only an education in formal is required.

According to Jim Rohn studying in a formal setting will give the student a job, while education on your own can earn an impressive amount. Les Brown, a well-known public speaker, was deported from his school following a diagnosis by the school as "mentally retarded." But that didn't stop him following his goals and pursuing the way to a dream. Les became a well-known communicater and also earned a steady salary doing something he was passionate about.

Learn about the lives of accomplished people. It will be clear that these incredible people's personality, dedication to work, habits, persistence as well as their ambition and dedication--rather than the formal education they received makes them stand out.

Billionaires such as Richard Branson, David Murdock, Henry Ford, Mark Cuban, Bill Gates, Mark Zuckerberg, Steve Jobs and many others renounced their studies to pursue their passions and build profitable businesses.

Why a College Education Does not Guarantee Success

Although formal education is important but a degree from a university isn't enough to assure success or extraordinary achievements. If you're looking to lead an enviable life, it is essential to have an ideal attitude and set of values. Sometimes, the best teachings come from personal experience more than from a college or school. Success or failure will depend on our capabilities of self-reflection and our capacity to be able to adjust to changing environments.

The perception of a person can be a significant determinant in the degree to which they achieve success. The goals and aspirations you have for your life do not depend on the educational level you have. If you're a college dropout, you could have greater goals than someone with a bachelor's degree. It doesn't matter what your education level is on your goals or dreams.

Following graduation, which kind of company would you prefer to be employed by? There is no doubt that you'll want to make applications to well-known firms such as Microsoft as well as Apple. It's true that these firms were started by entrepreneurs. In addition, the drive and determination are not influenced from your schooling level. You are not "qualified" for entrepreneurship; more of an "calling" and "passion" that determines one's whole existence.

This is why someone who has not completed formal education at an institution can still be successful in their career. It is possible to achieve both commercial and professional achievement.

The Value of Formal Schooling

It is important to recognize that formal schools and gaining a college degree can be beneficial to the world before you make any choices. If you don't have a formal education, it's sure that human beings will never be able to learn to write, read or even do math. In order to advance humankind and create the world a better place the need for education is vital.

The distinction between what is acceptable and illegal and illegal, is an important aspect of education. It is generally accepted that formal schools will reduce the criminal rate. A student who has completed their college degree is more confident and has a greater hope for a secured in the future.

A formal education also offers you the knowledge and skills necessary for working within the world of work. That's why educated people have a distinct benefit over those with no knowledge because they're educated and don't need to start at the beginning.

Most undergraduates in the opinion of Kevin O'Leary, a wealthy Canadian businessman, do not know the benefits they'll get through their education and therefore make large loans in a blind way. They falsely believed that they would be able to find work and then repay the loans when they earned a college degree.

If you're looking to make a bright life and fulfill your dreams it is essential to take the long-term view. You should have a clear vision of what you want in life, rather than following the crowd. While formal education is important, it is not a guarantee of the success you desire since your mentality, belief systems as well as behaviors continue to have a major impact on the success of a person.

What are the best ways to calculate the degrees?

If they don't have a wealth-oriented or other significant family, the common person requires assistance to get advantage in their lives. We'll go over the particulars of dealing with institutions and colleges.

The educational process at universities can help you expand your perspective and help you learn about various things about the world. To ensure everyone from different types of lives can benefit from the course's advantages, a common course of study is in place so everyone can choose the courses that most best suits his preferences while learning the fundamentals of various other crucial aspects.

The ability to master all skills and gaining proficiency in only one or two are crucial in our ever-changing society. If you look at it this way it is evident. If you don't, then it's because you're using the wrong lens for examining the finer aspects.

Dropouts is another phrase that's popular nowadays. Many individuals, such as Mark Zuckerberg, refer to themselves as "dropouts." They did however, not go to any college; instead, they went to Stanford, Harvard, and other top institutions. They received admission to the universities in recognition of their talent and dedication and thus have the rights to participate in any manner they want. However, you on contrary try to find an escape route from having to take responsibility for the fact that you have been denied admission to every reputable college that you had applied to. It's not the same footwear.

Strategies for Making It Without a Degree

A lot of the world's top business people, which comes as a shock, did not finish their college education. Dropouts from these schools are today one of the richest individuals in Silicon Valley having founded successful businesses. Even though their successes opened the doors to earn the fortunes they have earned even though they did not have a formal education in college The idea of what it takes to be a successful college dropout is perhaps more uncommon than we think.

The stories we read inspire us since they prove that anything can be achieved. Many people, inspired by these great historical figures claim that university education does not need to be as important and argue that it is counterproductive for the goals of an entrepreneur. However, does this constitute a deviation from the norm or is it merely the latest standard?

The section below will look at the experiences of those who failed to complete the college degree and discover what was it about their circumstances and backgrounds that enabled them to be successful. This information will show students who are considering dropping out that they could still accomplish their objectives even without the benefit of a degree from a four-year institution while being a warning for those contemplating leaving college altogether. For students who have chosen to not pursue further education and still desire the success they desire, this section provides tips on how to go about doing this.

There is a consensus among academics and researchers that taking a step out of school is an option alternative to a reckless reaction to an event that is stressful. The early school dropout could result from a mixture of school and student-related factors. The decision of each student to leave college is different, in the same way as the variables that affect how successful a dropout's decision will be differ for every individual.

The decision to stop earlier is based on a change regarding the costs or the benefits of learning as per experts. Additionally, "during the implementation phase, the student's engagement with the college environment alters the impression of numerous costs and advantages," the study states. When students discover something that is new, they evaluate the way their area of competence is placed. This in turn influences the likelihood of a student to put in efforts and take the time needed to achieve academic and social integration into the school. A study suggests that students' fatigue is the primary problem of effectiveness on the part of the institution as the institution does not offer students sufficient guidance, support as well as the necessary information for making well-informed decision-making.

The number of students enrolled in fall for colleges in the U.S. dropped 2.5 percent due to the outbreak of coronavirus as per the research. If compared to the year the year 2019, this is an increase of more than 400000 students. However, the percentage of students dropping out of higher education was already alarming, at around 40% prior to the epidemic.

The Idealized Dropout

The amount of students in college who quit their courses due to the outbreak of coronavirus is a source of sadness. These inspiring stories of accomplished people who didn't get their degrees give some hope. Social stigma associated with the inability to complete higher education has decreased over time. The tale about Silicon Valley, including its flourishing businesses and money, have changed perceptions about people who didn't take up higher learning. But not every dropout will have a pleasant ending. The problem with this narrative is that it doesn't include the many of other factors that could contribute to the accomplishment of a dropout from high school who later achieved remarkable achievement.

In the study of eleven,745 United States leaders (billionaires, multi-millionaires, business executives, federal judges, politicians and CEOs) The majority of them

(94%) percent attended college but not just any college since fifty percent of them went to an institution of value in a research study released in 2017 that examined the reasons behind academic and occupational achievement that is high. Contrary to what many believe it is clear that successful entrepreneurs aren't usually high school or university graduates. The results indicate that the success rate in the case of college dropouts is less than 6 percent.

If you're looking to get out of college to pursue your passion for something that may be one day a lucrative company, be aware that it's not an assurance of success. Many experts believe that a blend of connections, skills as well as a high-quality education are essential to succeed. Furthermore to that, there are a variety of characteristics in play that place an individual in a chance of becoming an entrepreneur, even if they don't have a education at a university, like naturally and with set characteristics such as ambition, drive as well as the ability to access resources and the ability to adapt.

Our Preference for Motivating Storytelling

The concept of a survivorship bias has been the main reason behind the enticing fantasy of the school dropout who is successful and distorted our perception of the extremely prosperous businessmen. Due to logical errors and cognitive biases, people tend to draw incorrect conclusions about the rest of the population based upon the extraordinary success that a select group of individuals who did not attend college.

These school dropouts that had a go at business in the face of poverty only to fail have been overlooked by this narrow attention to distribution. So do those who never had an opportunity to try the waters of entrepreneurship because of the shortage of funds. In trying to praise the person who failed to complete their the college degree, you must be aware that their lack of success or accomplishment is a consequence of an intricate interplay of influences, not only the ones we would like to focus on.

If you're one of the individuals who have had to pull out of high school because of the coronavirus outbreak or another reason, remember that learning doesn't have to be limited to the walls of a class. Numerous avenues and careers can be found. The first step is to decide upon a path to professional success and then arrange for the right education and knowledge. A different choice is to start a the business of your own. It's intriguing to see that students who drop out of high school actually are more successful in establishing their own businesses at a greater rates than graduates from college have. But, education is an important factor that determines the success of a business.

Chapter 3: The Dropout Mindset

No, this article is not about advantages of not attending the college. It's the "dropout mindset" is what is being discussed. Success of individuals such as Mark Zuckerberg, Bill Gates as well as Steven Jobs isn't due to their decision to leave the school before they did; instead they are because they have a similar mindset and values with the people who were also dropouts.

The attitude of a person with the "dropout" mindset is characterized by an absence of fear when faced with dangers typical of people. You have a college degree, an established job, lots of cash, a cozy life and so on. The ability to be a part in a developer's summit, while not noticing your low class attendance can open up many opportunities and expose the most influential individuals.

That's it! It's not a good idea to believe that you can achieve success only through your academic or professional academic qualifications. The people who have experienced significant success are able to determine the factors that influence their growth.

Ability to leave when the ideal circumstance arises or when confronted with hostile behavior is a useful ability. This will provide you with the courage to fight unfairness.

There was a lot we learned from the recent decisions. As a response to the growing concern over the integrity of Facebook's posts, Elon Musk removed SpaceX as well as Tesla's official Facebook pages the most popular platform in the world. This is a perfect example of the attitude that a student who dropped out of school has as very well. Life's challenges are not enough to frighten Elon Musk.

Although Facebook could be able describe the average person, it doesn't have any connection to Elon Musk, or his creations. Elon Musk creates.

Naturally, this is an opportunity you're willing to be willing to. The amount of your success is determined by the quality of your choices you make. Furthermore, you cannot make an "calculated risk" for crying in your head. Each chance comes with potentially disastrous outcomes. Do you see a distinction in success probabilities between students who drop out of high school and college graduates?

Analyzing the contextual

First-rate billionaires are significantly more likely to complete postsecondary studies over the average population. Additionally, there's an increased chance having an advanced degree in comparison having no formal education. This is not a great way to spread an idea that entrepreneurs are taught on the job and achieve success due to their own natural abilities and creativity, not the formal learning process. It is clear that 76% percent of those who are wealthy hold university degrees. About 47 percent hold bachelor's degrees, 23 percent are master's students in addition to six percent who have an advanced degree.

Institutions and subjects that are popular

Classes in engineering and economy were the top-rated classes. Students were more taking part in science-related programs than students in the humanities and arts combined. Additionally, those who are wealthy internationally tend to go to top universities than the state ones.

The U.S.

The United States, Harvard University as well as Harvard Business School are more likely than other universities to be mentioned on profiles of billionaires.

There's been a surge in the amount of tech-related billionaires with their roots in educational institutions like Stanford University and MIT. Sergey Brin, the co-founder of Google has attended Stanford's Graduate School of Business.

Russia

Moscow is among the most sought-after universities to these individuals with wealth including Moscow State University and Moscow State University, and a number of Moscow specialist institutes. This is a reflection of the increase in Russian wealth.

United Kingdom

Cambridge and the London School of Economics make the biggest single collection of British students according to this listing of multibillionaires. While Rupert Murdoch attended Oxford, Oxford is the Ecole Polytechnique in France has created more billionaires than any other college anywhere in the world.

Germany, Switzerland, and Italy

The billionaires have been spotted in the alumni of top institutions like the ones in Karlsruhe, Milan, and Zurich.

India

The majority of India's richest grads of The University of Mumbai, while steel titan Lakshmi Mittal attended St. Xavier's College in the city where he excelled during his studies. While in school, Mukesh Ambani spent time at Stanford University.

Numbers Don't Lie!

There are people are able to achieve success even without completing their college degree however, they represent the exception and not the norm. Marissa Mayer, Jeff Bezos as well as Sheryl Sandberg are only some of the most successful tales, and our research of education and talent shows that the majority of them are graduates of college.

The proportion of graduates from colleges in the top 1% of wealthiest and most powerful was looked at through "the conversation." The study looked at 11,745 of the top American top leaders, which included the world's top business leaders, global leaders billionaires, multi-millionaires Federal judges, politicians and CEOs.

Furthermore, the amount of graduates who attended "elite schools" was looked at. In order to be precise that we did not limit our scope to 8 Elite Universities. We also regularly included other top institutions of higher education and art schools where they are frequently ranked prominently within American News' best colleges for students in the undergraduate category and top schools for graduate ranking.

Ninety-four percent of these notable Americans were in college with half going to top colleges. Although almost everyone went to university but the number of students who attend prestigious universities is different. More than eighty percent of Forbes top 1% of the wealthiest people were educated at a top university however only 20.6 percent of the members of Congress and 33.8 percent of 30 millionaires have. A higher percentage of senators (41 percent) than congressmen went to Ivy League universities.

A study conducted done by Adview U.K. job site Adview revealed that 1 out of eight of the 4 hundred highest-earning

Americans had not completed high school. The reason for this was based on analyzing the educational background of the 335 and sixty-two billionaires to whom this information was published and discovering that 44 dropped out of high school. It confirms what was found in previous research conducted of Forbes. 16 percent of billionaires listed on the 2017 list do not hold an associate's degree in accordance with the research.

Prerequisites for Success

The following are the requirements to be successful:

* Skill/Effort

* Luck

* Unfair Advantage

The definition of hard work is putting forth efforts despite the obstacles that come your way, learning valuable knowledge and skills by experimenting and trial, persevering with your goal until you've reached the goal you set. In the words of a popular proverb, "Luck is when preparation meets opportunity."

The luck of the draw is in the event that God provides you with life-changing opportunities. The unfair advantage is crucial However, the three factors are skills that anybody could improve with time and practice. But this, in turn, is the most important difference-maker. There isn't a uniformity for everybody, however there are some universal principles:

1. Your Brand (MIT as well as Harvard alumni)

2. Your Group (Circle of Alumni Entrepreneurs, Investors)

3. Special Capacity That Sets You Apart

4. Family History

Chapter 4: Billionaires Who Left College before Graduating

Many people, if wanted to know their opinion, will tell you that to become a millionaire and be wealthy, you must be a graduate of an accredited institution to put in your collection. It could be the case for certain people, but there's a handful of people who seem to have everything they need to make billions with no education background.

The process begins with the idea of a vision, and this idea develops into a plan that leads to a successful company, product, or even an organization that makes the owner or creator rich. Some millionaires didn't complete their schooling. Students have enrolled in their college journey, then put in years of study, later quit in pursuit of their goals. Then they've amassed significant wealth to themselves. Below are twenty extremely wealthy individuals who didn't graduate from the college. Some of the names could be known for you, but the other names could be an unexpected surprise.

Howard Hughes

In the discussion of the most wealthy people living in the United States, Howard Hughes is one of the most famous people. After his father passed away, Howard Hughes was among the most well-known. his death, he quit college to pursue his passions. He was one of the most wealthy people in the world because of his accomplishments. He truly was a person with a variety of skills like the world's most prominent philanthropist, anaviator filmmaker, director and engineer. He also was an investor and businessman. His film-making efforts at the 20s caused controversy. Hell's Angels, Scarface, The Racket, and The Outlaw were just a few of films that were highly acclaimed and caused an uproar in the film business.

Marc Rich

Marc Rich has a wide variety of reputations. His history and his name have been criticized as illegal and controversial. He attended New York University before becoming an entrepreneur, but he left the school following a short period of time to concentrate on his position with Phillip Brothers. Before being arrested by the state on charges of racketeering, fraud on wires, tax evasion, as well as negotiating unsound oil deals with Iran at the time of the Iranian hostage crisis, Rich made a fortune as a commodities broker, the manager of hedge funds, financial advisor and a businessperson. Rich was living in Switzerland when he was indicted. the charges and never stopped his attention from in the United States. Rich received clemency from Bill Clinton in early 2001 and has sparked controversy. In a coincidence, Clinton's last day as president fell on the same day the pardon.

Ted Turner

Ted Turner attended Brown University and earned a bachelor's diploma in Classics and resenting his father. Turner changed to economics, and was then dismissed because of his wretched behavior when he was maintaining a female in the dorms of his college. When his father committed suicide, Turner inherited his father's billboard firm. His illustrious media venture began in the year he turned 24. He established and controlled numerous broadcasting networks, such as CNN as well as Turner Broadcast Network, which helped to make his fortune. Also, he was the owner of the MLB baseball team Atlanta Braves.

Ty Warner

The brand name Ty Beanie Babies has become synonymous with cute little plush toys. In the time when it was the Beanie Baby fad was at the height of its popularity, Ty Warner, the business's founder and the proprietor, reported that the company made $70,000 in just one year. The highly adored and loved small toys made a huge impression. Warner was a student at his school, the Michigan Kalamazoo College before leaving to go to Hollywood to pursue a acting profession. Warner moved to Chicago again and resumed working at the toy company Dakin after his engagement as an actor was cancelled. He established his own Ty Beanie Babies company after a period of twenty years in Dakin. Since the time, everything has been great for him.

David Murdock

David Murdock has gone from the beginning to something. The 9th grade dropout was recruited into the military during World War II, and after the time of war, he stayed in the streets, and needed help. Murdock was a man with the motivational stories that you read about. He was a tenacious man who earned his keep as Murdock kept on going. In 1980, he had been the biggest shareholder of Occidental Petroleum following his acquisition over International Mining in 1978. The value of his personal assets was estimated at around 3 billion dollars as of 2011.

Donald Newhouse

Even though he was a high-school student who dropped out, Donald Newhouse achieved success. Apart from Vogue, Conde Nast, The New Yorker, and Vanity Fair, he and Samuel and his brother are co-owners with Advance Publications, which publishes several magazines. In addition, they produce several newspapers within

The United States. The man is among the most wealthy billionaires and has a 4 billion dollar wealth.

Mickey Arison

Have you had any experiences about Carnival Cruise Line? Mickey Arison, the owner of Carnival Cruise Line, is accountable for the experience you had when you've been on a cruise on their ships. Because of his ambition to run and own his private cruise company Arison was interested in attending the university, but ultimately opted not to go. Additionally, he is the owner of Miami Heat in the NBA. The wealth of his personal fortune is nearly 6 billion dollars.

Steve Jobs

Even though they could barely afford it, Steve Jobs' parents put aside their savings in order to send their son for a trip to Reed College, Oregon. After nearly one hundred and eighty days in Reed College, Jobs left but kept going to calligraphy classes, while residing in a room shared by a fellow student. Then he established Apple as one of the most popular brands of computer technology. He credits his background in the field of calligraphy to create the wide range of fonts utilized for the MAC. He was Pixar's as well as Apple's Chief Executive Officer as well as the company's owner.

Jack Taylor

Shortly after registering as a student at Washington University, Jack Taylor quit because he wasn't enjoying being bored in boring lecture halls with dull lecturers. He walked away to concentrate on his other passions. Taylor was previously discussing investments however he was talking about to use them for making investments in oneself, rather than the business or college. In the end, Taylor did exactly that which made him one of the most wealthy people on earth with a few billion dollars being attributed to him, as well as continuing to run the rent-a-car company that's producing a lot of cash.

David Geffen

Due to his dyslexia problems, Geffen left Santa Monica College after which he was offered a job as a mailroom clerk for the William and Morris Agency. Then, he became the head for Laura Nyro, Nash, Stills, and Crosby following his decision to pursue to work in the entertainment business. In 1970, he created Asylum Records, a record company which housed the likes of famous musicians and artists. Geffen owns the record label. Geffen has signed artists such as Linda Ronstadt, Tom Waits, Bob Dylan, The Eagles among other artists. In addition to DreamWorks SKG and Geffen Records He also runs DGC Records.

Ralph Lauren

As the owner of one of the most renowned clothing brands in the world, Ralph Lauren, Ralph Lauren does not require any introduction. He attended classes in business over two terms in Baruch College, but he quit the following year. After two years of serving in the military between 1962 through 1964, he became a salesperson at Brooks Brothers until opening a necktie store and launching his own brand of tie with the name Polo. There was no formal training in the field of fashion. All was that he had was a solid character and talent to design and create clothes. The company is worth $7.5B due to his clothing and accessories company as well as many years of success.

Michael Dell

When he was a student at University of Texas, Michael Dell began a tiny startup business in his dorm room. After creating computer upgrades kits, Dell finally was granted a vendor's license which allowed him to make bids for the construction projects that were in Texas. Low-cost "no-overhead" bids were Dell's top bid. It made sense for him because his residence was in a dormitory and had no overhead. Dell eventually decided to stop the studies in order to concentrate on the tech industry, and today, through Dell's Dell firm, he's made a wealth that reaches several billion dollars.

Sergey Brin

After the announcement of his and his partner's idea for the company now referred to by the term Google, Sergey Brin left his studies for doctoral with Stanford University. Sergey Brin and his colleague Larry Page conceived the idea of creating a search engine which would connect users across the globe in real time. The software became a huge success that brought him to the top of the list with a value in the billions. The software, in turn, legally dropped out of the conventional school despite not having even know it was part of the doctoral degree program. we think he'd agree that the decision was certainly worthwhile.

Larry Page

Along with Brin, Larry Page and Sergey Brin piled their Stanford dormitories with their supplies and went at work on creating the largest search engine ever created. After leaving Stanford and moved into a the garage of a lease in order to develop and finish their idea. They created the famous Google that is used everyday to browse through the internet and go between pages. We wouldn't have been here, or even know how to do with Google.

Mark Zuckerberg

Have you heard of, or registered for Facebook or has the site? 3 of Zuckerberg's Harvard University undergraduate friends and who he worked with to develop Facebook. Businessman, computer programmer and of course, the chairman and CEO Zuckerberg is estimated to have an estimated net worth of 43 billion dollars. He left Harvard to pursue his dream of Facebook and is currently among the wealthiest people due to.

Kirk Kerkorian

Due to his partnership in the form of his collaboration with Martin Stern Jr., Kirk Kerkorian has been one of the major individuals in the growth of Las Vegas. The three times he was involved, starting in the year 1969 by constructing The International Hotel and the MGM Hotel then followed in the year 1973, then followed by in '94, the MGM Grand in '94, Kerkorian built the most luxurious hotels that were built around. The major world-renowned philanthropist Kerkorian has donated to Armenia over one billion dollars via his charitable foundation. In the year he died in 2014 his estimated worth was $24.9 billion.

Sheldon Adelson

The resort, casino and hotel industries are the areas where the businessman Sheldon Adelson is active. In the past, he's established more than fifty of his own businesses two times becoming millionaires and not making their fortunes. When he was just twelve the founder of his initial firm that sold newspapers. In the following years, he began marketing the substance that defrozes windshields. The total worth of about $29.8 billion in 2020, he's one of the top billionaires on Earth as well as the owner of the well-known Las Vegas Sands Hotel and Casino.

Lawrence Ellison

Prior to leaving due to the passing of his adoptive mother, Lawrence Ellison briefly attended the University of Illinois. Then he stayed for a short time as a student at University of Chicago. University of Chicago before leaving. Ellison is a businessman, and co-founder of Oracle Corporation. Ellison has developed software for major companies and institutions. With a $36 billion fortune and a love for sailing, he's also created his own yachting company, known as BMW Oracle Racing. BMW Oracle Racing.

Bill Gates

Prior to recently, Jeff Bezos, the creator of Amazon has held the title of top-earning man in the world. He surpassed all the billionaires listed in the rankings. Gates quit his college studies to start Microsoft which has since become the most profitable software firm. The foundation he founded along with his ex-wife assists millions across the globe. One of America's biggest philanthropists Gates his life's purpose is to give away the majority of his wealth to help improve the world, especially for those poorer. He's already given more than 47 percent of the wealth as of now, and is planning to increase his giving significantly when he dies. The man has a 107.2 billion dollars net worth.

John D. Rockefeller

John Davison Rockefeller had an estimated net worth in the range of $392-$663.4 billion (in the present day dollars) prior to his passing, making the world's richest man in the world. The name of his has become to be synonymous to "wealthy," which he was able to achieve through creating a firm giving, saving, and a strong work moral code. Along with his brother biologically, William Rockefeller, he entered the industry of refinery and oil as well as some of the facilities later was the largest oil facility anywhere on the planet. Rockefeller achieved the status of being the richest person in the world without any college degrees.

Jay-Z

The rap star Jay-Z, "Money Ain't a Thang" is quite true, as he owns billions! Jay-Z is real name Shawn Corey Carter, began singing as a kid in order to escape the drugs, crime and despair in the Marcy projects in Brooklyn. The rapper even left high school in order to get into drug-dealing but he rethought his decision after his mother gifted him with the boombox which ignited his passion for music.

The Originators The Originators is a track that Jay-Z and Jaz-O released in 1989 was a hit on MTV. Then Jay-Z began to go by"Jay-Z" on stage "Jay-Z," which was an amalgamation of his personal moniker, "Jazzy," and the name of his teacher.

Jay-Z created Roc-A-Fella Records in the 1990s the music label which was able to sell more than one million albums of his debut album across America.

Alongside the wealth he has earned due to his career in music, Jay-Z has a sizable portfolio of investments, which includes holding a stake in New Jersey Nets of the NBA as well as an urban-themed apparel brand, as well as a chain of bars that are sports-related.

Evan Williams

What does Medium, Twitter, and Blogger have in common, aside from the fact they're all very popular blogging or microblogging platforms? The person who founded both of them are Evan Williams.

Williams was born on the family farm but he's always longed to run his own business. In 1990, he was enrolled at the University of Nebraska, but the following year, he resigned to concentrate on his business. When he began the podcasting venture and he met Jack Dorsey. They started working together in the development of a messaging program which was launched in 2007. In 2007, they founded Twitter.

Compete.com included Twitter among the top social media platforms at the time that Williams was its chief executive. Williams promptly resigned his position, however he continued to be a passionate advocate to be an entrepreneur. Then, he launched the online blog platform Medium at the beginning of 2012.

Chapter 5: Ten Traits of Billionaires That Make Them Successful

The fact is that an entrepreneur's mindset is an asset that's worth having - it will help you accomplish everything you'd like to achieve in life. It's not necessary to come from wealthy families to be able to enjoy an attitude of millionaire. Anyone can acquire the attitude that a billionaire has by following the following first: Understand that money doesn't mean everything. The true billionaires do not focus on how much wealth they own, but rather the importance of their money and its impact on their lives as well as those who surround their lives. The second is to learn to be present in the now. If you're always looking ahead it's more likely that you'll make the most of opportunities presented by life. Don't think that money is the only thing that defines your worth

Remember that there are a lot of people that are equally competent as you in becoming millionaires.

It's been said that being wealthy implies that you're an unreliable puppeteer with zero weaknesses and an unfathomable nature. This is what makes you a guaranteed success. This isn't the reality, particularly in the case of making it a billionaire. We don't possess the knowledge of finance or money necessary to establish enterprises, or invest in innovative ventures, or become financially secure.

Most of us have a tendency to spend money but aren't able to handle our finances efficiently. That isn't to say that every person isn't able to become financially secure and prosperous if they've got certain qualities. Take a review of some most common characteristics that billionaires possess. If you adhere to these guidelines and follow these guidelines, you'll be well on the path to achieving a millionaire mentality - an ideal goal for everyone!

They Set Goals

The most crucial characteristic that a person could possess is determination to achieve the goals they have set. It is essential that they be able to define the things they would like to accomplish in the future, how they plan to complete it and in what way they plan to achieve it. If you are looking to attain your goals, you should have the plan of what you're looking to achieve and the reason you'd like to accomplish it. If you're not sure of what you want to accomplish then you can be able to get there by meticulously making a plan for your journey.

They're Self-Disciplined

People who are successful have the discipline to realize that they can't accomplish everything that is feasible. The things you have to accomplish, you have to do. Things you should avoid is something you should avoid doing. The most successful people are aware of what they have to do however they are also aware of the things they should avoid.

They Must Be Willing to Work Hard

The need to work hard is a standard feature of billionaires. They aren't able to afford regular pleasures such as social gatherings, or being part of the market. They work all day to grow their business and take on new ventures and make themselves financially secure. Actually, the greater your success and the greater effort you'll need to work for the results you desire. This is similar to the old saying which emphasizes the significance of dedication. Work is not done without getting paid.

They Know How to Invest

The most important thing to do in order to become millionaire is investing your funds wisely. There are numerous ways to make rapid money, however they are often wrong. Make sure you invest your money correctly to ensure you can get a good yield from your investment.

It is a way to invest in investments that offer high rates of return. The best way to accomplish this is by investing in stocks. Stocks are investments that offer the potential for a large amount of profits because they're either mining or buying companies. If you do not have the knowledge to invest, then you need to be educated. There are numerous sites and books that show you to invest.

They Have Good Networking Skills

The most successful people are able to build relationships with successful individuals. They have the ability to interact with successful people within their field and gain knowledge from the best of them. This is perhaps the most essential quality you could be a successful business owner or investor. It is essential to know how to build relationships with fellow entrepreneurs, investors as well as corporate executive.

If you aren't sure how to make connections then you need to master it. In addition, you should master the art of networking fast. The most successful people are able to make connections and build friendships with people they like. They are also able to establish Business Networks and create strong relations with other entrepreneurs.

Intense Focus

Millionaires are people who understand how to invest all their efforts into work. They aren't prone to socializing drinking, having fun, or engaging in other things that can hinder them from achieving their goals. They meticulously plan their day in advance, what they'd like accomplish and the best way to go about it.

The most important thing is that you must have the desire to work hard. If you're not willing to do the work and work hard, you'll never accomplish any success. If you do not want to be a hard worker and put in the effort, you'll never be prosperous. The key is determination to achieve success because that's what is required to be the next billionaire.

Takes Massive Action

The most crucial characteristic a individual can possess is the need to be proactive. What's the first thing that pops into your head when you think of "action"? If you're like many people, the answer is probably not the financial freedom or even a good enterprise. The more successful you become and the better your chances of success, you'll need to act.

It is essential to make sensible and thoughtful decisions since the money you have isn't some magical liquid that flows into or out of accounts. It is essential to make choices which will result in results since the money you have isn't a static matter that grows up on trees. It's not just a money that you could spend as you please. It's a resource with a limit that which you have to manage with care.

Can Negotiate

Every successful person knows how to bargain. They are able to negotiate for less than they'd like for an item that is more valuable or give more than what they're worth to obtain something that is less valuable. If you're not able to negotiate, then you have to study.

It is important to become proficient at giving and taking lesser than you would like to obtain an item that is more valuable or it is necessary to learn how to give more than what you are worth to receive something of lesser value. There are numerous negotiation methods to help you negotiate the most favorable deal you can get. All it takes is understanding the business language and understanding how to get the amount you are entitled to.

The Perspective of Failure is Different Among Billionaires

If you've lived under some rock and you're wondering why the billionaires didn't fail were the ones you created. People who are wealthy are also prone to making errors. The trick is to adopt a new mindset and looking at the failure as an opportunity to learn and grow. Take the time to reflect before attempting with a stronger determination.

A billionaire's mindset involves thinking of failure as a place along the way which will let you refresh so you can go on instead of a roadblock that stops you from going on forever.

The person that is first thought of when thinking about the richest people in the world are Bill Gates, or much in the past, Elon Musk, who is an excellent example of this mindset. Elon Musk was not a billionaire from birth. He dropped out from Harvard and not only other institution, but the high school and college. In addition, his company was alleged to be a victim of theft, and required to be unable to process in traffic.

In the present times, we don't think that, even if he arranged the cost of everyone's education at college however, he'd be able to afford enough cash to sustain his lifestyle. You can celebrate a win However, it's important to take lessons from losses According to the man.

It's crucial to follow the example of Gates and learn how you can efficiently transform your mistakes into wins, while celebrating your accomplishments.

Seven Ways to Create Habits That Last

Do you look over your schedule and realize that there's no way to get everything done? Perhaps you're feeling as though you're never enough that you can't get time to do things. In either case, it could be difficult to find the drive to keep an exercise routine. It doesn't matter if you're trying to shed weight, give up smoking or develop new habits We all recognize the importance of regular exercise to achieve results. However, the challenge lies in establishing activities that can be sustained which means that actions aren't as a burden, but instead are enjoyable routine.

It's not easy to create habits this is the reason why a lot of individuals give up after several unsuccessful attempts. If you have the proper skills and a little creativity there's no reason to stay like this.

For a better experience Start thinking about the habits you are practicing as full-time work. This is that you must achieve your goals, rather than giving up after failing a couple of times. In that regard these are the 7 Habits that last to help establish new habits that last for the long haul.

Make the habit loop

A habit loop is an action which you do time and time. As an example, you get up around 6:00 in the day, then you head to work until 5 pm, then return home and rest until you're into a deep sleep. But what happens if choose to suddenly add nutritious eating habits to your routine? If you're not vigilant it's possible that you'll end up taking in unhealthy food and feeling ashamed all day.

A habit loop is an action you perform that you repeat repeatedly. As an example, you get up around 6:00 in the day, then you head to work till 5:00 at night, you go home, and lay down until you are into a deep sleep. But what happens if choose to suddenly add nutritious eating habits to your routine? If you're not cautious then you could end up taking in unhealthy food and feeling guilt-ridden throughout the day.

Place it on the floor and observe the result.

The first step to developing habits that will are lasting is to actually put your new routine into it. If you can do that then you'll set yourself to be successful. As an example, when you choose to begin an exercise routine that you've never done before it's not a rush into full-on sprint. Instead, you slowly increase the intensity of your workout then, within a short time, you've made great strides. This is the same for creating habitual patterns that will last.

Begin small and gradually progress to the next level. This can help you avoid the frustration of not making improvements at the same time. After you've created the new routine You'll need create a schedule to keep track of your progress. It can be as simple by saying in a loud voice or writing the words on a piece of paper "I'm going to start eating healthier tomorrow."

Keep Going When you're Feeling Weak.

When we start new habits, it is common to be too ambitious and attempt to achieve too much fast. This is an error that lots of people make, as it is a recipe for failing. What's important is to push yourself constantly, but don't go too far. Find a way to strike a balance between being a challenge without feeling as if you're doing it too often.

It's one of the most efficient ways to avoid exhaustion when you're trying to develop lasting habits. If you feel a bit uneasy, push your limits a bit more than you had previously. This can help you remain motivated and feel as if you're progressing. However be careful not to take yourself too seriously and you'll risk burning out. If you do this, you'll end up feeling worse, and you'll have less motivation.

Build Habit-Respective Environment

One of the easiest methods to build habit that will last is to establish a respectable habit atmosphere. It is basically about setting up your surroundings to support the new behaviors you are trying to establish. As an example, you can get some nutritious food items or locate a way to display them around your house.

One other thing to consider is create a spot in which you can break when you have to. This can be a comfy place in your house or even an designated break area at work. This can help you stay away from overtraining, and provide you with the opportunity to relax in times of need.

Understand Why You Want to Change

One of the best methods to establish lasting habits is to remain determined. That means you have to be regular in your exercise routine and making healthy food choices. What is essential here is to be constantly motivated to continue to work out.

One way to accomplish this is to discover some aspect of your new routine that you enjoy. It might be the sensation of satisfaction you experience when eating better or the way muscles feel following exercising. It can serve to keep yourself in a state of mind to push yourself to keep going following your new routine.

Do not damage the chain.

The most important habit to keep is one that a lot of folks do not think about. This is not to damage the chain. That means, when creating your new routine be sure be sure that you're making sure you take care of the old ones. Although this may seem odd initially however it's really crucial. If, for example, you're working out every day it is important to care for your mental health too.

That means you have to figure out a method to calm yourself when you're exhausted. It will prevent you from burnout and will also help make sure that you're taking good proper care of your mental health. This can help you keep the chain from breaking and will increase the chance of establishing habit changes that will last.

Keep your eyes open to yourself.

The final habit that will last is one that most people do not think about. It is to be honest to your self. In the process of creating habit-forming habits that will last the longest, this is one of the most essential habits to create. That's why you must find ways to be truthful to yourself with regards to sticking with the changes.

This could be as simple as jotting down your goals or letting them be spoken in public. It will allow you to remain consistent and prevent you from falling off course. Also, you should be mindful in judging your self. The result will be low motivation and negative emotions. to keep going.

Have a short break once in a while.

The final habit that is long-lasting is one that a lot of are unaware of. This is to take a break occasionally. It may sound like a lot however it's one of the most effective habits that you could develop. If you want to create lasting habits it is among the greatest habits you could be able to.

It is important to regularly break to break from the new routine. This helps you keep yourself energized and rejuvenated as you're working. It will help you prevent burnout, and to avoid getting off course. This helps stop you from breaking your chain, and increase the likelihood of developing habit changes that will last.

Most important to keep in mind is that changing your habits takes time and effort. You have to work hard to develop habit changes, and efforts to keep these habits. However, the good news is that work produces results and if you stick with the process, you'll begin to notice outcomes. Actually, putting time in developing habit changes that will last will help you create a stronger, better healthy you.

The characteristics that successful billionaires have in common are self-control, workaholic driven, goal-oriented, driven, diligent and persistent. Anyone with these characteristics could become a millionaire. If you've got the right qualities and are willing to work hard then you too will be able to become a billionaire. What you have to do is follow these guidelines and follow them in order to be wealthy.

The Real Reason Why High School Dropouts Outperform College Grads

It's that time that grads are celebrating their newly earned degrees, and families throw parties in honour of their children and wear gorgeous caps and dresses for pictures. There are some who have jobs set and others remain in uncertainty, not knowing which direction their future career would appear as. What exactly will life be when you graduate? What is the real-life value of this achievement in any way, in comparison to other options?

The majority of people we know who have found their way toward fame and success began out with nothing beyond a handful of abilities and qualities. Nowadays, the majority of businesses would travel heaven and the earth in order to find an applicant who has these qualities and skills. They tend to look on their own rather than looking outward. Being aware and in control of who you are.

A majority of people have realized their imperfections and are utilizing this recognition to go further and reach even higher levels of success. Whatever your area of study You'll require these qualities to reach your objectives. Learning gained through their training and usage is far better than any other academic qualification.

The natural abilities and efforts of the human body are in conflict.

It's not obvious that the vast majority of new graduates suffer from Post-Graduation Syndrome. It's hilarious because it's an obvious indication of the reason that many graduates are unable to find a job that is satisfying within their fields and find themselves in a job that isn't worth their time elsewhere. Graduates of colleges are hopeful that they won't have to exert a lot of effort since they possess the skills necessary to succeed in their lives or lead more happily. A false assumption is that a college degree is the magic bullet which will propel you towards successfulness.

A research that was conducted by Silicon Valley at the beginning of the year found that a shocking 70% of engineers, designers and programmers employed at Big Tech Giants such as Facebook, Google, and Apple aren't armed with an undergraduate degree of four years.

Yes, they're graduates. Because of this growing understanding many tech giants have taken college degrees off of the job descriptions of their employees.

Don't be the graduate who believes that he or she isn't required to study and learn or develop in any way because they have everything they need or want to be completely content. You can be that dropout who recognizes that nobody has the expectation of any thing from God and works hard to make improvements through regular studying, exercising and experimentation.

As a bright and intelligent man who knows that to succeed then you must create yourself a chance and overcome your own personal boundaries without relying on any other person.

Unwavering focus on success

The college experience is an accepted norm within our culture of today, that's why most students are pressured to comply with the rules. College may be a good option for certain individuals, but it will not be the best choice for the majority of people today. In fact, today information is accessible because of technological advances that have greatly shaped our modern society. The achievement of this was impossible only a half century earlier.

What is the key to success is an emotionally invested in the work you're doing. It was discovered that the success rate can be measured in terms of grades in the college. However, while it's accurate however, it fails to understand what real development and growth entail. Being compelled to take part in a particular activity due to the fact that it is something you think you should do be successful is not uncommon during the college. It is impossible to do anything; the community you are living in tries to make you slaves. In order to avoid getting penalized for not obeying their rules, it is best to quit the programme.

The flipside is that having a low GPA provides all the benefits which a degree from a university does not.

True financial freedom, according to "20-Hour Workweek" author Tim Ferriss's theory may be unrelated to how much money you've earned. Nowadays, true financial independence is the ability to use your time however you like with no obligation to anyone else but you. Being able to set your own path in life and pursue a profession you are passionate about is unbeatable. Genuine

Perseverance, perseverance, and determination

The actions taken by college students as a result of academic requirements as well as group assignments and the pressure of peers. The students rarely make the effort after they have achieved their goal, it's typically theirs for the taking. It's similar to cramming your final exam over the course of a weekend, and having no more use for what you learned. It's not identical to doing research. When things become hard, college students either quit quickly and switch into a different direction, or find comfort with alcohol, parties or even sexual activities.

If you're working towards an objective you're deeply passionate about, you'll persevere regardless of what obstacles come to you. Because it's something that you look for with excitement so it's not a burden to working. Right? According to research that was published in Harvard Business Review, about 82% of people's "extraordinary" qualities come from their persistence. It's the case of dropouts who decide to create their own business. They can surpass expectations without a doubt or reluctance.

The passion to work

The skeptics tend to focus on the notion of being successful. The people who do amazing things are the ones who put their best effort into the method. The tendency to lose sight of the present and now, instead of thinking about the failure and loss of the guarantee for the future. If you ignore everything except for the details and procedure it is possible to live fully within the present. One wise old man declared that a person who's admitted defeat and disappointment and shows no signs of slowing down should be our biggest fear much more than the reflection of the mirror.

If you believe to the method and trust in the process, you stand greater chances to achieve your goals. A daily commitment to the smallest aspects will help you set yourself up for success in the future.

Have you noticed that people who are working really intensely often fall short, and those who do not seem to have any concern for the end result generally get it right? This is the reason specifically. A decision based on the fact that success, though likely, but it's not guaranteed. It calls to abandon all hopes. Instead of adopting an optimistic outlook the following is to be in tune with traditional realistic thinking. Politicians and business executives tend to be portrayed as having the same world view.

The road to success appears different than it appears through the lens of media. It is not always achieved by direct means. In reality, there are many patterns of zigzags. The dirt and rough surface conceals the fact that it's neither gorgeous and an aesthetically pleasing. There is a lesser-known fact that golf balls that have the highest damaged and wear are the ones with the fastest launch speed. It's how the pathway towards success often appears it'll take place. The jokes aren't as funny now that society has transformed to become something completely different.

Chapter 6: How to Have a Billionaire Mindset: Tips for Becoming A Rich, Successful Person

Ever wondered what it's like having a millionaire's mindset? How could your life be transformed in the event that you can accumulate money over time and create the wealth you desire? It's true that having optimism about your life, being grounded and making plans for the future are essential elements to becoming wealthy.

According to the old saying it is impossible to make money just by being poor. This is particularly true with regard to becoming an entrepreneur. What does it appear like? Is it necessary to have an silver spoon inside their mouth?

There isn't a manual or plan to become rich. If you adopt an appropriate mindset, any person will be able to overcome their challenges and achieve financial freedom. These sections will show how to become a millionaire to transform your circumstance into wealth.

If you're looking to accumulate wealth or increase your financial security We're here to share strategies to assist you in becoming a wealthy well-off and prosperous person. The tips below can help you get there sooner rather and not the time. Learn more about what it takes having a billionaire's mindset as well as how you can begin making money, and how to prepare to be a successful, rich and well-off individual.

Create a wealth-building foundation

However many billions of dollars you accumulate in the end The only thing that remains yours forever is the foundation that you create of riches. It is essential to create a culture in which saving money becomes an everyday habit. It is essential be able to keep a tight control of your finances and set up a process set up that allows the savings to be consistent.

The only way to effectively prepare for the future is getting ready for the future. Once you've got a good knowledge of your financials it will be possible to know precisely where your money is getting. Additionally, it will enable you to establish financial goals for yourself in order that you feel confident regarding the coming years.

Make plans for the coming future

Making plans to plan for your future can be essential due to a variety of motives. Most obvious is it can allow people to save money. Many people go through the pay checks every month but don't take the time to think about precisely how they're spending their funds. Once you've started making plans for the future it will be easier to determine where your money's being spent.

It will help you manage your financial situation in order to accumulate an even greater amount of wealth, and be financially secure later on. One of the most important methods to be prepared in the near future is to begin making savings. Many people do not believe that it is necessary to invest money in savings, but this is among the most crucial actions you can take to plan to face the challenges of tomorrow. This will help you accumulate a greater sum of money, while also ensuring that your financial situation is steady in the long run.

Network, network and network!

One of the easiest method to make money is to locate a wealthy person to assist you in becoming financially secure. What's the reason you would do this when you are able to make connections with rich people via the web? One of the most effective strategies for gaining wealth is to meet wealthy individuals and ask them to assist you in becoming financially sound. There are millions of millionaires in the world who would love to get acquainted with someone looking to improve their financial position.

Connecting with wealthy people and having a wealthy friend who's willing to coach you is among the most effective ways of creating wealth. It is possible to get advice from them, and also inquire about any concerns regarding the subject of money. It's one of the most effective ways to become wealthy because you will be able to meet wealthy people to aid the financially. You are not only making yourself richer however, you're helping other people as well.

Develop emotional intelligence

Millionaire mentality is one that is powered by the power of emotion. It is essential to know how to read people's behavior and assess their mood. This can help you make better decisions in making financial decisions, and will help you improve your understanding of yourself.

You'll better be aware of your emotions as well as that of people around you. This can help you make more informed financial choices, and also to recognize the emotions you feel when experiencing them.

Be organized and flexible.

As you get more financially secure, it is essential to keep your financial affairs in order. That means you have to have a plan set up to track all of your activities and find out exactly where everything is. Once you begin to become financially secure, it's essential to stay on top of your game.

This allows you to remain focused in saving money, and to build the most substantial sum of money. It will be easier to remain well-organized and save money once you begin to become financially secure. It will help you keep your focus in saving money while building an even greater sum of money.

Make sure you are a happy person.

When you're positive in your mental attitude, it can help you to grow into a better person. That means you have constantly work to improve your self-esteem and becoming the most effective person that you can become. As you get more financially stable, it's crucial to keep working on getting better at yourself and becoming the most successful person you could become.

You will be able to improve your character and live a more satisfying standard of living. There are many actions you could take to be a better individual and enjoy a higher standard of living. One of the most beneficial things to do is keep working on getting better at yourself to become the most successful person you can possibly be.

Avoid wasting time in boring tasks.

It is important to not spend your time doing things which are not productive. It is important to concentrate on things that can help you make money. One of the most effective methods to be financially stable is to work on creating wealth.

If you begin focusing on creating wealth, it will enable you to be financially secure. There are numerous items you must be focusing on when creating wealth. If you begin focusing on the accumulation of wealth, it'll allow you to be financially secure.

If you're able to have an attitude of billionaire that you're living at the present and start looking forward to the future. Each day as a chance to create wealth, and be financially secure. You should not spend your time doing nothing but passive things. Do those things that allow you to accumulate money in the near future. By doing this, you'll be more financially secure later on.

Chapter 7: leaving College with success

Students who've had to overcome major challenges through their lives, share certain characteristics, despite the fact that they have distinct personalities. Many may see these successful individuals as having quit too early however, they compensated the gap in their academic training with a fervent determination and determination. These guidelines are applicable to everyone and could help you when you decide to make a change in your lifestyle.

There's plenty to gain from researching the lives of successful dropping outs, no matter if you're at school or taken the plunge to give up your education. Keep in mind that your decision today can have ramifications over the course of the next 10 years or so.

1. You should be able to discern the direction you are heading

How and when to quit college or high school can differ widely from one person to the next. Some students decide to skip their education at university to pursue a career in your own business, or even joining into the workforce. A few people already entrepreneurs opt to put off academic studies for the sake of committing themselves entirely to expanding their company.

Nearly all of those who've had success dropping out of college did this with a clear and flexible business strategy. Based on the reasons you're abandoning college, you'll have determine the next steps and whether you can actually do it. Think about the advantages from having an emergency strategy.

2. Design a network diagram

Access to the resources you require is essential to be able to move freely. What is the stability of your relationship? Do you have your role models? Are you connected to anyone with whom you could serve as investors in angels? If you are looking for work or setting up a company it is vital to network. Each field has its own ecosystem which is why it's important to surround your self with those who are knowledgeable about.

Mary Gates, Bill Gates's mother and an entrepreneur who has made a name for herself by herself She is widely acknowledged for the introduction of her son to IBM's chairman at the time, John Opel, in the 1980s. This was a crucial step to the success of Bill Gates within the world of computers. The rest is an interesting story. John Opel and Mary Gates were both as members of the United Way Board.

3. Recognize your best assets

Do you have a clear idea about what you can sell? How do you do well? If you have an amazing idea for your business, you'll need to know how to bring it in action. It will require the proper combination of minds to develop your idea, and then nurture it into a mature. There's no need to do much other than jump around and have your buddies to cheer you on. Stories of success stories from people who did not finish their college degrees illustrate how vital that you are capable of coping with uncertainties.

4. Make money for your savings.

Make use of online free classes and other resources to cover any gaps in knowledge you be able to fill in with your knowledge collection. Business professionals who are successful but did not graduate from college are among not the only ones to say that those with higher education have a higher chance of success in their business ventures. Each person's mind is different. So, college isn't an ideal option for everyone. But we should accept the challenge to learn all throughout our life. The motto of the innovative post-industrial, post-industrial business can be summarized as "upskill or perish."

5. Accept uncertainty and be prepared to fail at times

If you choose to quit the school you're taking a huge risk however, you must prepare for the possibility of more. People who managed to be successful when they dropped out of school didn't shy away from making a gamble. Be aware, however, that these were not risky bets, but came about through careful analysis and preparation.

The people listed above are able to tackle complex problems, even without university degrees. Their achievements in academics could be traced back to their many years they spent at school. Similarly, don't let setbacks deter you. Steve Jobs has remarked that losing his job was the most satisfying experience that could have ever been experienced by Steve Jobs because it forced him to begin from scratch and make a comeback.

6. Return to the school.

The benefits of having a college degree is still valid. About one million former dropouts from college earned their degrees in the last academic year. The successful dropouts were students who later enrolled at the schools. In fact, even

Gates who is a self-made billionaire who did not complete his high school now aids students to pay to attend and pay for colleges. It is impossible that high school dropouts can compensate for their lack of experience on the job market following an entrepreneurial route.

The college experience is often referred as "life's first endurance test," which is why students who have passed the test are given a greater degree of respect as compared to those who didn't. The college experience can pave you to more prospects and help put your resume on the top of an employer's pile.

The trade schools and professional certification programmes can allow you to gain an edge if school isn't an option. Consider how the cost of healthcare is growing at a staggering amount and that the trend won't stop any time in the near future.

So, it is possible to profit from certificates within this field. Medical coding, dental assistant and billing certification courses are two of the most competitive online certifications. It is best to save funds to attend school when you start earning a good income.

7. Dropout rather than Freethinker

In a sense it is true that the stories of students who quit school has changed our perception of people who opt to skip an education that is traditional. The experience of these students can be motivating for pupils yet it does not make the degree earned from an accredited school of higher education outdated. It is important to remember that the value of an education will never be lost. A well-known Silicon Valley native who did not go to college believes that the present tendency to minimize the value of education is not necessary as it doesn't consider factors such as social class and ethnicity.

It's your decision to determine what you want to do following our outline of the traits shared by successful people who have opted to skip universities. Contrary to the popular opinion it is important to look for and seek advice from mentors as you create your own course. Make mistakes, but be mindful of how important it is to keep positive relationships. It's not difficult for brave people to cause hurt; be cautious.

Look at the common traits of every college dropout who has had a long-lasting success regardless of whether they chose to start a company or choose a different path. It is essential to take a method of measuring success, one that considers the success and failings. The examples below of how you can be a top-performing dropout share some commonalities which make them effective.

There are some schools that can take your classes completely online. This means that you could go back to school and continue at it if you want to. Be determined to achieve the goals you're aiming for and education is not all you need to accomplish it. Always keep in mind the end goal Life begins when you graduate. Create a strategy for your own development and learning. Keep an open thinking. There is a chance that you could become the next top-performing student if you have the determination, competences and talent, as well as the desire to ability to adapt, and, perhaps foremost, the right networking.

Learning to Rise Before the Sun Like a Billionaire

It is possible to train yourself to be a step ahead of the sun, and gain an edge over others. If you can learn to prioritize effectively, you'll not just achieve greater results in less time as well, but you'll also have a better physical and mental wellbeing. If you're not able how to manage this behaviour and you'll find yourself doing more and longer and never getting any results. The majority of the world's accomplished businesspeople start early.

It's a given that the most successful people on the planet as well as the most successful business leaders--many of whom we've had a pleasure of meeting, or even reading their works--do things which are unique from the way the majority of people perform.

They are also the first to rise. This is why many of those with the highest esteem in corporate management have a higher rise than the majority of the population according to our personal experience of well-known billionaires Fortune 500 CEOs, and entrepreneurs.

Billionaire businessman Richard Branson, the owner of the Virgin Group, starts his morning with an exercise routine in the 5:45 a.m. Jack Dorsey, the co-founder of Twitter is an early morning person who gets up at 5 o'clock to do a meditation session and run six miles.

Jeff Bezos, founder and the CEO of Amazon starts his day early at 5:30 a.m. Both Apple as well as Disney have founders and CEOs that are young: Tim Cook at 3:45 and Bob Iger at 4:30. Former CEO of PepsiCo, Indra Nooyi, is frequently referred to as one of the world's top 100 women. In contrast to Howard Schultz, Starbucks' richest CEO, who wakes early at 4:30 a.m. Indra Nooyi is up by 5 a.m.

The Philosophical Stone

The habit of waking up early has been touted as a secret weapon for productivity by philosophers throughout history.

Aristotle said that it's beneficial to rise before dawn because these practices can result in health, wealth and intellectual ability. There is a claim that Benjamin Franklin remarked that sleeping earlier and rising early makes one wealthy, intelligent and fit.

Many German proverbs stress the importance for waking up early in order to establish the right tone for a successful day and a happy existence.

The German proverb "The early bird gets the worm" is translated into English to mean "The early dawn has riches in its mouth."

Early risers have many benefits

People who rise earlier can be more productive, have greater mental well-being and greater energy during the day than people who stay in bed. The most obvious advantages of waking up earlier than everyone else will allow you to complete the most important work of your day completed with virtually no interruptions.

Why is it not a better alternative? The ones who are most important and need your complete concentration. One of the factors that make the process so effective is that it's very difficult jobs. If you are able to get to this state of mind and focus, you'll succeed and achieve the best results achievable.

A long-term commitment to work can bring significant benefits. Not the labor-for-labor's-sake company that characterizes most folk's life. There are likely to be extended hours of leisure time. Peter Drucker, the "father of modern management" and an eminent management specialist during the latter half of the century, stated that the extended hours serve as the base of any significant impact that an executive can have.

Huge drain, little benefit

If you're a business owner or an executive, then you're aware that it's crucial that you take your time for the best results. Progress can only be achieved this manner. It's not like you're an assembly line worker doing nothing more than a series of meaningless tasks all day. You currently hold an office of leadership. Set an example for others and arrange your schedule in the way you prefer to have others arrange yours.

The ability of you to accomplish this is greatly enhanced if you start your day early. When you get your most significant job done is an immense boost of confidence. This is an motivational boost that can make the rest of your day look manageable, even enjoyable.

These are the steps you can take to aid you to get up early

1. A timer set for the evening instead of the early morning that is most effective.

It is important to set your alarm for evening time rather than the early morning. What exactly would this mean in the first place?

Cut your day's time in a way in order to wake in the morning. If you fall asleep at the appropriate hour, which typically around 10 p.m. You can wake up around 3:45 a.m. at the majority of times and without the need for an alarm.

If you extend the time you go to bed, you won't have the energy to get up when you wake up. It's your responsibility to experiment with a few different time limits at night before you settle on your ideal schedule. But the key, however, is paying more attentively to your nighttime alarm as opposed to the morning alarm. You should go to sleep as soon when your alarm ceases to ring in the midnight.

2. Following a consistent routine to go through before bed can assist you in getting comfortable and winding down.

The same thing has been mentioned many times in the past, it's worth to be reiterated: top-performing individuals regardless of the industry, field of work or industry, stick to their unique routines to ensure they are successful in the many different areas of their lives, where the efficiency of their work is essential. Nighttime routines are an example.

There's no need for complexities there. For a start it is recommended to study the habits of others who are accomplished people on the internet. The idea behind this exercise is to assist you in winding down after your workday and be ready to face the day ahead. The routine for your night doesn't need the time of an hour. Instead, 20 to 30 minutes ought to suffice.

3. Restorative power nap

There is evidence to suggest that if you have short naps throughout the day, it will require less rest as compared to if you did not nap in any way. For instance, suppose the typical daytime sleeping schedule is comprised of 8 hours of uninterrupted sleep. If you add on the additional of one hour's rest it could be the 6 hours you need to sleep is the minimum you require.

Bang! It's like you've lost one hour of sleep. If you get to sleep, the faster you'll be awake.

Chapter 8: They Made Them Highly Skilled

It is clearly an vital ability. From the time they were children, they've done things others might not have thought of. They have tried to improve their talents. But they didn't have the time to read any books, and they believed they'll succeed in the near the future. Let me ask you this question. Have you ever had the experience that you were reading something on a ability or other, after which you stated that you would take it up in the near future or that you would like to master this skill again in the future? Perhaps it was about learning something new about skills that you already have. It is likely that you answered yes to this particular question. This happens a lot of occasions that people learn something new and declare that they'll try it. If you don't have the ability to accomplish things today, you won't be able to perform it later on.

Tomorrow will likely remain the same as the present. Accept that the conditions of tomorrow for you to are effortless. However, the moment you discover that is more if you begin at a later time. The amount of time you spend will be higher when you start early, however in the second scenario, it isn't advantageous. Let me give you a scenario A friend and you would like to know how to play Football. The two of you learned about it, and then thought you would try it in the time, however the friend you played with started to play the game. It wasn't something you tried in any way, you simply said it might be in the near future. Later on, you realized that you got started.

It is rare that you begin doing things that you put aside for a future time. It's extremely rare, however, just be sure you have done the right thing. It was then easy to start for you. It is possible that you will soon be doing decent dribbling. You may also play with more strength than at the age of your youth However, you'll need to work on it. Perhaps you're thinking about the person I recommended. It is a sport that you can master however, do you have the thought of competing against your friend. It is a sport he has played at a very early time, so he'll surely become an expert in the game. He spent a significant amount of time to get his ball under control and he spent a great deal of time shooting with the power of a gun, he required some time to get it in the right place as well as do all of that earlier. However, who's the best player? Do you think that you will ever be a part of international Football matches?

Don't expect me to provide the solution for the question, it's simple. However, you should ask yourself the reason for this incident. The reason is that you didn't finish your work to tomorrow, and you were with a friend the same day. Thus, learning something during childhood requires time. However, if you do exactly the same thing for a long time you will see your performance increase several times later on. There is the J curve to your performance, but this does be the case for adults.

These successful individuals who we're talking about have been highly proficient since when they were young. They were always working to improve their skills and enhance their skills. There were many failures in their youth, but this was to be enjoyment. When they began doing things professionally, they did not make mistakes because they knew exactly that they knew what they were doing. If you've done something a thousands of times, will you ever be scared to attempt something outside of college?

It was the same with everyone. They'd been through identical things a number of times, so afterward they were not worried being unable to do this after they had left the school.

Imagine you're an excellent debater, what do you feel scared going outside your school for debates. There is a chance to win, but what will you feel nervous while talking? Are you fumbling? Do you begin to stumble? If you've been through this in college or at school several times and think you're good at it, you should have no fear. The feeling of anxiety at the end is not the same as fear when working on something. Therefore, they weren't afraid of failure at work however, the outcome is always on the shoulders of God.

It was not uncommon for them to create things using their talents as children. They didn't think about once they got a work, they would be able to utilize their abilities to create something. They always were driven to create something using their abilities even today. they were responsible and took charge of things. There was never day to come, therefore whatever you would like to achieve, you must be doing it now. Below are several examples:

In the early days, when Mark Zuckerburg was just a youngster, he displayed his enthusiasm for computers. His parents saw this interest and decided to purchase computers and weekly his teacher came over to help him learn the basics of computer programming. Parents could pay for it to purchase it for their child. The tutor began teaching his computer programming. After that, he developed a software known as Zucknet to help his family. Zucknet comprises two words: Zuckerburgs and Network. This greatly helped the father of his. As a dentist, colleagues would not be shouting for the next patient. In the beginning, he was young and it was not the final word on his activities.

Elon Musk was only nine when he began reading the manual for computers that would accompany all computers at the time. The guide was read to gain an understanding of computers. However, it was his passion to create something with the help of his father, that he developed his own game for computers. The game was later sold to a business at a price of $ 500. It was a child however this didn't hinder him from doing what he wanted to do. He was a prolific reader as a result of this only. He was more avid than other people at his age.

In this moment, I feel I'd like to tell you some facts concerning Warren Buffet. It is likely that you are aware Warren Buffet is an excellent investor. However, what I really liked about him was that he first began investing in stocks from a young age. It was his first investment at the age of thirteen years old. Is it true that a child of 13 made a bet on the market for stocks. The thing I love more is that there was a chance of losing money on this investment, yet he continued to invest. He purchased 3 shares for just $38. The price of the stock was purchased began to decrease. He began to feel anxious, which is not surprising, as it was all that he owned. After a few days, it was $40. Then he immediately sold all his stock. In the following weeks however, the price went up by about $250. In terms of technicality, he did not suffer the risk of losing money, but it was clear that he'd suffered an emotional loss. He learned about this before investing by thinking in the long run, and now He is among the top investors around the world.

I've got many more however they're all in this book. So keep studying. My conclusion is crystal clear up to the present. They've always been working hard in their abilities and have given some time for this. They don't have time for foolish orthodox studying. I said orthodox as we aren't sure what we're studying about and we're just following the other students, who are following other people in turn, and then being a part of us like other people. The whole process was done for very many years, and today we aren't sure what we're studying. It's just to earn an education, get an occupation, and then do go about it. There is no intention to study something. It is important to know the reason why be studying and what do we need to study? It is my opinion that the what we study will depend on the individual, and is different from one individual to the next. The subject will be addressed at the end of the book, but until then, I'd like to believe that you already know this because it is described in the whole book.The additional point about the reason why we should be studying and going to school is also going to be addressed at the end.

Chapter 9: the read Many Books on Numerous Topics

Now, I'm asking you, how many books have already read? The most important thing is the textbooks and other side-books in any field must be omitted from this. Tell me your response. If I asked for you to not read any novel or storybooks, then what's your solution? No, I'm not going to discourage anyone from reading tale books or novels. They are very beneficial as they aid to develop our vocabulary. Then there are other types of books that help us develop our thought processes. This includes biographies of notable individuals, and books that are related to the topic you love (on whatever subject or the one you wish to pursue is the same subject, but on a greater quality, in which case there is no way to get scores) Encyclopedias, and the encyclopedias. What do you think? If you've provided your answer, then you can search the web to find out how long these people with whom we're talking about read?

The children read their books every day. They would read for hours to improve their knowledge. The books they read did not just focus on one subject and were covering diverse subjects. The reason they read was desire and did not want to gain anything out of it. In the beginning, they did not intend to earn money, however later on they would always use it by their. They were extremely passionate readers. This is why I'd be happy to share a couple of stories, and I would like you to understand why do I intend to convey.

Elon Musk was a fervent reader since a young age. From the time he was born, he had been obsessed with reading. How many books can be found at the library of your school? It is likely that you do not know however, he did read every book at the library. Are you able to believe it? you read every book at the library. He then asked the librarian to provide more books, so they could be read by him. He enjoyed reading books on diverse subjects.

The evidence is within the businesses he started. Many of you are aware that he's the chief executive officer of Tesla as well as Spacex or concerned about his work in SolarCity as well as OpenAI. Do you realize that he also founded many other businesses, which I'm not sure of in this article. I've already mentioned that he invented an app that he later offered to a business at a price of 500 dollars. He then created a website known as Zip2 it was similar to an online Map. He then sold the website and later launched a new site called X.com that is for accepting and distributing payment. A similar site was launched near to them that took their steps. This led to the two businesses being were merged. The new company was called PayPal. This is, in fact, the PayPal which we currently use. Then, it was transferred to eBay.

He then started his own company Spacex due to the fact that he was unable to find cheap rockets. So it was his goal to lower the costs of space travel by developing Rockets that could be reused. The idea was born but on the flip side, he invested in Tesla since he believed there was a the future of this firm. The company was creating something that could revolutionize the world in his opinion therefore he decided to invest there. At that time, Tesla did not do very well, so he was made the company's CEO. He then invested in SolarCity since he was convinced of the future of SolarCity.

You can see what broad subjects the presenter is engaged in. What is his method of accomplishing this? It is done since he is knowledgeable about the subject matter. He gained that understanding through reading books, book, and more books. Also, I'm hoping that you are aware of the value of books. In this article, I'd like to present one small instance of an amazing persona within the next sentence.

I believe that the majority of you have heard about Bill Gates so I want to present some of his tales about his love of reading. From the time he was a child, he also a reader. He enjoyed studying books. He also enjoyed one other aspect he was passionate about which was using computers. He once was disallowed the usage of computers by his parents as they were concerned that they were sending their son in the incorrect direction if he spent his time in the computer center until midnight, because computers were huge and could not be put in homes. In the end, instead of crying the front of them, he opted to accept. It was so easy for his. After that, he started to read books every day.

There is no doubt that you have seen parents discipline their kids for not doing their homework or giving them instructions to do their homework. In the case of Bill Gates it was totally different. Bill Gates was extremely interested in studying books. In fact, he was obsessed with them, that he would bring them around the dining room table. He even forgot to eat during that time, so the parents would not allow him to take books to the table. He was an avid read.

Do you think that all of them had a passion about reading books or anything else. However, suppose you also quit your school and the texts you are studying or the understanding that you acquire from the subjects covered in them, will never be a part of your brain. Are you aware of what I talking about? Start reading and learning about various things.

In reality, the purpose behind this book isn't to tell you that you won't be successful even if you quit. The purpose of this publication is to inform readers the reasons why they were successful, and the steps you can take to succeed. If you are able to comply with their strategies, then likely, you'll also be successful. Remember, however, that I'm saying that you follow their steps rather than copying the steps. I'm sure you get it.

It is my opinion that it needs to be made clear. When I say follow, it means that you must adopt good aspects of the book. It is recommended to adopt the practices that are described in this entire book. It isn't my intention to replicate exactly the same thing as they did. They took the right steps in the moment. However, the time has changed. might be that step that worked at the time doesn't work in the present moment.

Bill Gates started a software business at age 20. He was extremely success. However, if you can do exactly the same thing, will you succeed? Let's look at the forecasts. Software can be classified into several types generally: Software for systems and applications. Microsoft mostly made available operating system software Windows that falls under the first group. You may have already used Windows and are planning to change? If a brand new business offers a new version of their software, and you decide to purchase the software from the company? Maybe not because you already have an excellent product.

If software is great, nobody will purchase it from your company. What if you could make it more effective? They employ thousands with huge funds and everything else they'll need. How do you get the amount of resources you need? In the present time. To become a leading player in the market is a huge challenge. How then did Microsoft got its foot in the door?

In reality, Bill Gates and Paul Allen(his co-founder) realized the possibilities of computers. They also realized that every person could be producing computers. They would therefore require powerful software that could be used to create a fantastic hardware. Thus, they forecasted the technology of the future. There were not any software firms providing truly excellent software that was easy to operate. So, they marketed Windows and were so popular.

What follows Bill Gates is to try to look ahead and find what's lacking on the market. Do your best to make life for people more comfortable as he did by creating an excellent machine user-friendly. In other words, copying Bill gates is to simply without even thinking about it, you can quit school and develop a program even if you're not a pro at how to code. This is the way I'd like to talk regarding following the footsteps of these individuals.

Chapter 10: They Started While Studying and Then Dropped Out

This seems obvious, and I'm certain that many of you are aware the fact that they began creating their dream projects within their colleges only. Many even used their university resources to launch the project. Mark Zuckerburg hacked his college servers, and obtained photos of every student. After that, he launched his site, FaceMash. It is the foundation of his instruction for Facebook. The website you visited were presented with photos of two individuals and the user was asked to pick one as being attractive and the other not. The site gathered large numbers of teens who utilized this site. The website even utilized the servers at his college to maintain the website's availability. Due to the high load, servers weren't able the same level of performance as they had previously. In the end, college demanded Mark to explain all of it. As he does today, in the aftermath of the scandal on Facebook Mark took on the burden for everything, and the college offered him a second chance.

However, the issue that was a problem with FaceMash even after gaining thousands of users was that a few people began to disliking the app. They were dissatisfied due to the fact that they did not get the same hot status again and repeatedly, and they began moving away. If this had maintained, then users could have kept returning and wouldn't have had the huge user base that Facebook has. The company learned lessons from the experience before launching the company.

Every billionaire who has a dropout are following the same path. Bill Gates with

Paul Allen began his business at university solely. The computers at the college were used to design a software program that would run on the most recent microcomputer Altair 8800. The team created the program together after which Paul Allen went to their offices to present them with the program. They were impressed with the software and the concept extremely. Then Microsoft began as a separate business to develop software. The company soon was taken over due to poor performance. In the year 2000, Microsoft became an independent company. However, when he planned to begin all this, the company, he submitted a leave request to the school, however it was a few years later that he came back to be awarded an honorary degree from the university. One thing to remember is to remember is that at Harvard University, you can be absent for any time to return. This is a wonderful.

It should be apparent for you to know that they didn't leave in order to accomplish something. They decided to expand their business. They had great ideas to change the world. They had also created their own businesses that had been doing well, and that could be growing significantly in the near future However, only if they pursued their ideas seriously. They believed that they had the potential to create huge companies. Like if someone told that you were the winner of a lottery ticket that will be won and you've decided not to buy the ticket. The lottery ticket was a gamble, and regardless of the outcome the chances are they'll have the experience and skills to land the best job. It is necessary to have a degree in order to be eligible for an entry-level job. However, once you've completed an occupation, you will be called upon to prove your experience and abilities. Therefore, they had both of these.

They were floating in the sky. They were able to fall at any time. They tried to remain there but they did not. If the worst could happen to them the chance of falling. However, if you crash from space, you'll most likely fall upon a large palm tree. The tree is there in just a handful of seconds whereas others need many years to get there. location.

This is a clear indication that they were not going to pull out at any moment. They had no intention of dropping out but were compelled to do so. Nobody outside was pushing them, but their circumstances had them in a position of force. I've told you before that they had been working on something massive and was growing quickly. The 2000s were a time when you might be aware of the speed at which the internet was expanding. The growth rate was averaging over ten times every year. The data from surveys showed this. In other words, if you were in their workplace, could you quit the organization that worked towards something that could transform the entire world?

Yes, my answer is no. I would like to hear that yours is as well. If the answer to this question is a yes, then please do not try to offend, but you're not able of reading this book. You can read stories for children. This isn't saying this to say that you're not smart, but simply because you're not part of those who have the ability to learn these books. If you study the stories of your kindergarten, then you can change your mind. The reason is that the morals in the tale are easily understood by your. This can aid in forming the mindset to go through the book.

In other words, if we're able to make a correct choice, then how could make a mistake in that situation, which would ruin their job and family's prospects, and also can they lose out on the possibility of helping millions of people around the world. They made the difficult choice of leaving however not in the way that some people believe. The company only submitted the application for absence, but the situation was different for of Steve Jobs. This is expected to be covered in future chapters. I'm expecting it'll be included in case I forget to record it.

The reason they quit was that they were compelled by the circumstances, their company as well as the need to aid everybody and to transform the world better. They didn't feel happy making this decision. They did their best to not to leave. Sure, they tried to leave. They attempted to work as well as study simultaneously, but their work was gruelling and studying required classes that took up all their time. You can see the difficulty. If you're a college student, then studying may be extremely difficult for you. And if you're a worker in a workplace, then you might be aware of it is a struggle to live your life. There isn't time to unwind or make the time to be with your family, and you may not have enough the time to take care of you. However, they attempted to accomplish both of these things. The work for the firm was growing continuously and the size of the company was increasing. The company was not able to even consider of reducing the growth rate to allow them to finish their education and be able to do more work once they have graduated.

The whole thing was ruined because of the thought process behind the competitors. The field in which they were in was incredibly competitive in that moment. Therefore, slowing down could mean destroying the business and giving another chances to transform the entire world. How do you accomplish this in your opinion?

It's very simple and obviously, no one would be trusted, and so they chose not to. Finally, they quit. You would then discovered the reason they left but they also became accomplished. The story isn't over. There are many more astonishing aspects that will help make you think and reveal how successful they were. The illusion of luck out of your mind and show that they are lucky. Some people believe they had success early However, I do not believe that. If you're interested to find out why, read this book.

Chapter 11: They Had a Dear Path Of Future

I've shared with you many aspects of their lives. They were employed to earn money. as children, they read many books. However, does this by itself result in this level of success that they had? It's true that it's unlikely since this success is just too huge. Their achievement is huge enough and everyone else isn't able to achieve it. The question is how did they attain this level of success despite leaving. It is possible to give you a single sentence answer, but before I do I can do that, I'd prefer to talk about what it is like to are always learning about college. It will be simpler for you to comprehend the reason why these business owners became this prosperous.

If you're a students, then it should be easy to grasp. If I asked you what your college or university would like from you, then what is your quick response? Perhaps you're thinking that you must study diligently, for knowledge, or achieve success in life. Later on, however you'll hear that you need you want to score scores. The goal is to score high marks in order that when you quit, other students will join because of the larger number of students. Certain colleges are not included in this, because they aren't doing the same thing, or don't have the need to. It doesn't seem like this is the reason behind Oxford University or Havard university or any other. They've shown their talent to all, so they do not want their students to earn good scores only. Instead, they would like to see their kids confident and productive in the future. That's why Harvard offers its students the option of taking any length of leave they would like.

If someone who is studying to obtain scores, what's the mindset of that person? The student just wants to know subjects until the exams aren't finished. And then he doesn't want to reread that book. It's just a wish to achieve high marks. The best aspect is that the colleges support this. They would like to see higher scores. Thus, a smart child can be focused on his studying all day long (believing that he will not be a cheater). If he studies every day, where do you plan for the future? When you consider thinking out of the college system, or about the future, then these students are tagged as bad pupils. Many people aren't interested in such labels, so they'll try to do their best, but they will fail.

Do you depend to get a job at the university because of your high grades? If you are offered an offer from a excellent company and then when you reach the age of 45, you're the chief executive. What do you think it will take to have the same success the drop-outs had?

It's not possible to believe this. Even CEOs with the highest salaries were not able to achieve this level of accomplishment, especially if they're not founders of the firm. Sundar Pichai is the CEO of Google and Alphabet. He's a billionaire however, he is not as rich as the founders.

Do you know why it is why you don't achieve that achievement? It's because you are aiming for a tiny amount. In the day when you depended to get a job, you made a small-scale goal. The goal was met However, the success you achieved isn't huge because the goal was low. The knowledge, skills and all the other things you have are useless the moment. If you set your sights on small and then you'll never be successful since your efforts are reduced as you reach your goals.

You should set your goals very high so that you are more likely to fail than your peers successful people. That's a strategy is in their minds and they are still thinking about it. If that wasn't the case, Elon Musk wouldn't have worked more than a hundred hours per week at Tesla as well as SpaceX. He's set a ridiculous goal and is now determined to meet these goals.

There is no way to know what sort of job that you're likely to be offered You don't even know the company you're going to work for and you aren't sure if this company is right for you or not. what can you do to get ready to be ready for the position you'll be offered at the business? What do you do if you didn't land an employment offer? What should you do if you are offered an opportunity with a low salary? What do you do in the event that the employer decides to fire you immediately afterwards? Many more are present in my head But do you know which one of them?

You don't. It was unclear what you likely to be doing in the future. You didn't know anything about the future. That's because you weren't doing the things you wanted to do, but doing what people told to you to accomplish. If you do not want to strive to achieve your goals and others make your work harder to achieve their own dreams. You're hoping to live an excellent life and having a successful career, yet you focused all of your effort in studying in order to score high marks. Do those high marks aid you when your employer decides to fire them? Are those marks able to help you when you aren't able to get an increase in your salary for a long time? Do those marks aid you should you require money to cover the costs for your children?

Good marks can be very damaging. Let me share a tale about the boy who is named Harry however, isn't Potter but think of the character as you would and consider what you would perform in all of the locations.

Harry was a child who did well in school. Then his parents wanted to complete his graduation. He picked three subjects in order for his graduation. The college year starts in September and he excelled in school. He scored the first place in two subjects, but was 15th for the third. It was because the subject didn't appeal to him. subject very much. He wanted a job in the main area, that's Physics and the 3rd course was Maths. The college he attended recognized his talent and his instructors advised him to pay more attention to the third area, while their parents also advised him to do the same. Therefore, follow the instructions and concentrated harder on the subject.

The following results were announced with him being the first student in two subjects, and was fifth in the third. The entire class was pleased with him.

At the same school, He had acquaintances. They were all good at academics, but they were not as good as him. One of his buddies was Sam who scored 7th place in his first subject, and 29th and 19th in the second and third. Sam was among the least intelligent of the intelligentsiast group. He was also interested in pursuing an academic career in Physics However, he had never focused on his fellow students.

It was time to go on. the last exams were been completed and it was time to see the final results. Harry was the first to be awarded the top spot across all subjects. Harry's companion Sam received third place in the very first subject but has barely beaten him on the remaining two. They each applied for jobs in the same company. They both had to go for an interviews and both, several questions were given. They did both well in their opinion. In the end, Sam was picked while Harry did not get the job. There was only one few days since the outcome had been announced and nobody knew exactly how the whole thing took place.

In the following year, Harry was able to attend post-graduation and at the time, Harry was horribly confused about what subject to choose. There was only one course, so he got lost between Physics as well as Maths. He wanted an occupation in Physics However, he was convinced that by doing this, all effort put into Maths could be wasted. He finally decided to study Physics since he was able to score high marks, he believed. However, after his first exam however, he was unable to perform quite well. He was convinced that the answers were right. Therefore, he contacted his teachers and asked for the information. They informed him that his answers could be accurate, but they were related to other subjects he done his research and had paid lots of focus. He was beginning to consider about the subject, so the answers were from the subject areas. It was not about the topic he was learning about.

Let's say, for instance, you are doing research in Physics. What is the reason we should wear belts on our seats? This is because when we stop our vehicle abruptly, we won't force our bodies forward because of momentum. However, if you write it so that we don't get punished by the traffic police. The same could be the case however in different ways.

Then he realized that not just his efforts have been in vain and also that it has damaged his abilities in his favorite area. Then he realized why Sam was chosen for the position. In reality, Sam had studied a single area, which is Physics. What he did know was a part of Physics. He was a part of the Physics universe, and he believed of Physics. In the course of a conversation with Sam He came to understand that he didn't just study the syllabus, however, he also did more than just the syllabus. He did that since He was passionate about Physics. The rest of the world doesn't matter to him.

The firm wanted someone with a good background in Physics and did not care about any other subject expertise. So, they chose him. What is the reason he wasn't able to secure the first spot in Physics? Since he was studying something other than the curriculum that could prove useless at college, however, it is extremely useful in other schools. At that point, Harry realized this and focused on the areas of Physics which he was a fan of. Then he didn't pay time to other aspects. He was then hired by a company that dealt with aircrafts, that didn't seem to care about the subject matter he was studying. In reality, he utilized the knowledge he gained from other areas for his position later however, only occasionally. Being knowledgeable about other subjects can be beneficial, but the problem occurs when you have to pay for more than what you actually need.

There is a certain amount of knowledge that will be more beneficial to you. So, devote the subject more attention focus on it, and be more attentive. However, what Harry did was he spent more time on a area that wasn't as beneficial for his needs. He didn't maintain a balance. Sam was not a student in other subjects. So, it came time to know about Maths or Chemistry the subject was searched via the internet or talked to other people. While studying them at college, Sam had an knowledge of the subjects.

The outline that remains after a few years of study can be pretty much the same for everybody. No matter whether you're a topper or otherwise.

The information he acquired was the amount that was needed by his needs, and not much any more. This was good enough to have an excellent job. He gave the time and attention that was required but not any more.

Don't mean 'Don't take classes in other subjects'. I'm saying you must be focused solely on your knowledge. This should be as if you are giving all your energy to that. The knowledge is endless and if you or someone else thinks that we must know everything Then that person is a fool. There is no way to be a master of everything when you've lived for thousands of years. Your life is short therefore, focus on the things you cherish and consider what's important to you.

Harry could not be spending more time on Maths If someone had been there to impart this knowledge or to tell this tale. When you concentrate on the weaknesses you have and weaknesses, you will become an normal. If you are focused on your strengths, you will become the top in the entire world. Spend time in your thing that you're the most effective at. It is possible to leave out the areas that make you a failure If you wish, however I suggest you try to have fun with them. Consider them as a time-pass. They are definitely worth a small amounts, however with this method you won't be overwhelmed and will not care about the results. You're having fun while getting to know that subject. This is the way to find out what you don't find enjoyable. There is no need to be the top in this.

Therefore, I'm hoping you liked this story and come to be aware that college isn't always a good thing. They are looking to earn our favor. That's enough to let you know the reason why entrepreneurs like these are accomplished. They weren't looking to concentrate too much on things that were not important. They were taught things that isn't useful for them in the future. It could have been a part of their subject that they adored. Perhaps it was also the case that they had already known that due to their reading.

There was a plan in which they were involved and that was able to change the world. The project was likely to grow large one day if they believed. They weren't dependent on their job. They weren't dependent on a degrees, and therefore weren't dependent on schooling for a successful job. They weren't confused about whether this was a good thing, or what is best. They knew the way they'd go. Finally, they weren't going to spend their time or focus to any other thing. They were clear and had self-confidence.

The matter is taken serious and is embraced by Mark Zuckerburg and Steve Jobs as well as other people. It is why people wear identical clothing all the time. They do not want to spend their time and energy on selecting clothing, therefore they wear the same outfits every day. This takes little effort and time. And they believe it is unimportant. So how do they spend all their time doing other subjects that could have been used to study?

They were highly focused on their goals and the future. They even had the courage to correct themselves if they'd been mistaken in the past. Mark Zuckerburg had Psychology as his primary subject at the college. After he realized the error, he changed his subject in to Computer Science. They understood the next steps that needed to be followed by their organizations and also the actions that they had to take. The decision to leave was only a minor move, but if they had to make a riskier move that they could not be hesitant to take a step back. This is due to the fact that they were extremely enthusiastic and certain of the future success of the company. The reason for this was that the direction of their lives and their company was crystal well-defined in their minds. They were all extremely creative and visionary.

Chapter 12: They Were Working For Very Long Hours, Even For Nothing

It's a true that they worked to earn nothing. They were not willing to relax or were not interested in weekends. They weren't interested in holiday season because they were busy engaged in what they love. They worked for their achievement, not just for the celebrations. They realized that they were doing more work than they were required to be doing in their college but they pushed working. They tried to avoid this kind of thoughts as they can make them weak.

Their dedication and passion could not be matched, but the most significant thing to remember is that they weren't receiving any compensation for their efforts. They were employed by their own businesses, however they weren't receiving an income. However, this doesn't mean the business was not earning significant revenue. The company was even paying employees. It was earning money however, according to them, that was lower than what they were paying at the moment, could harm the business over the future.

They believed this. They paid their workers for their needs however, without salary they'd be unable to pay. They said that taking money from their employees at an important time in which the company was expanding, paying salary was a mistake. It was because the development of a company demands resources, marketing, and cash which is why instead of earning them, they were investing money to fund these activities.

They weren't looking to limit the pace of expansion by their naivete of money. They wished to invest every penny earned by the business back into the firm. They were visionary, so they saw that even a small issue today could lead to the difference for a better future, not only for themselves but also for the entire world. They could have cheated on everyone else by stealing much more than they are entitled to in the same way, but in truth nobody could ever ask a questions. They didn't need quick growth, they just wanted massive successes. They even gave up what they wanted for their company.

If they had requested this from their first employees, then they certainly would be denying. The employees all were looking for money, but not person was able to appreciate the possibilities of the business and accept a job for no cost. Free work isn't foolishness, but they could certainly have received higher stock options later. It shows the mindset of their employees.

In essence, this is the distinction in an owner and his employees. It is what differentiates visionary and non-visionary person. This is what differentiates an unsuccessful and successful person. All of them were employed at the same location, but how come only a small portion of them were able to see the potential of the business and not other? The reason only a handful of people were attracted by salary, but not other employees? How come only a handful of people wanted to make a difference in the world, while others simply wanted to complete their work and make cash?

I'm not sure if I want to share any more about this issue. That's the main difference between the two, and this could be the main reason why there is a difference between graduates and dropouts as well as their difference from us. True, graduates can't achieve this. Indeed, they have to spend lots of money for their graduation, as tuition. The parents of the graduates have invested in their education. It could even have taken out an loan in order to finance their schooling. This has become very popular in recent times. Parents often take loans to help with the educational expenses of their children. They believe that this is the most beneficial thing that they're taking care of their children but in reality, it creates fear and makes the parents not to take every risk.

In the next step, they must find the job they want as fast as is possible. After they have gotten a job, they have to make income. The need for a salary each month. They wish to have a stable life and show this through repaying the loans parents took out for their educational expenses. Sometimes, due to the pressure to make the repayments and due to pressure from their family, they pick an occupation that they quickly decide they later regret it.

Regret could be of various varieties. It is possible that they regret the fact that their firm is not doing so well since they dismissed him quickly after a meeting. The situation may appear to be fine for a child. It is possible that you can find a job in another place. If the authorities ask for work experience and the reasons why they left, there is a problem. The character certificate itself is problematic at this point. Therefore, they might regret they chose a bad firm.

Another reason to be disappointed is the fact that they were in such rush to get their job that they failed to look into the other job openings. The other firms that are better than the business that they're working for have a lot more advantages. They even offer more pay, a better workplace, as well as additional benefits. This may not seem like an issue, but it is disappointing. The regret is more intense in the event that one of your close friends is hired by the company and they praise the company constantly. The regret is even greater when you have a dumb buddy.

It is extremely hazardous. The reason for this is the fact that you do not receive advancement in your workplace. They have employed you over the last five years, and they've not offered any an important promotion. In the meantime, you've not learned much from them as they're traditional people who aren't willing to change and innovate in the current world. So how do you find an opportunity to work? It is not like you've learned anything that is new. You've forgotten everything you learned in school. (Make sure you are practical, and the majority of your knowledge was absorbed for you to earn high scores). This is why it's difficult for you to find a new job, but you're not getting promotions either. A second issue is that the business has not been innovating, and does not change in the current world. It could end up being lost at any moment. What do you do?

There are many regrets of doing a wrong decision in the hurry to repay the loan. What I recommend to parents is to send their children to lower school rather than making the children afraid of their future which means they are unable to make the proper option. A loan is like having shooting a bullet at your head. You are required to pay it off quickly.

This person could get the chance to interact with the people who have dropped out of the company about which we're talking about. The person will likely work for them, however his fear of having to repay the loan won't permit the company to refuse pay and request stocks options or other benefits such as those that come with the company expands. You and I don't have any idea of their skills, but my guess is that they won't be able to because they're scared. Fear has shut their eyes to wisdom and also has allowed them to open their door to more money.

Another issue is that many people are unable to join a startup. The reason is that an start-up company can't afford to pay their employees much and they'd like to earn more fast. They'd like to secure an entry-level job with a major firm. One possibility is they aren't. Are college graduates able to find a job at Apple, Microsoft, Amazon or Google? If they do get the top, will they be able to grow enough to be as successful by starting a business?

The potential for growth is greater in a start-up as it's smaller and once it grows, it will get promoted, and be able to grow. Start-up growth is quick and even a mature business can't keep up with the rapid growth of a great start-up or the level of growth it experienced at the time they starting out. However, a startup can certainly grow rapidly If you select the best starting point.

This is an important aspect that you must choose your options very carefully. If you make the right choice, you'll be able to succeed If you make a mistake, incorrect, your life could be destroyed. However, the alternative could be to make your startup prosperous. You might be able and intelligent enough to let them know what's incorrect and correct the aspect. It is essential to be a vital member of the company's start-up. It is not up to them to guide you, however you should demonstrate leadership skills at the same time. How do you feel can CEO, CFO and similar posts get being filled by start-ups as they get bigger?

The idea is based on how well the members can perform. So show your skills. However, if you were the one who started your own business, then you're not the person who gets selected, but you are the one who chooses. It is possible to choose yourself but you must analyze every person with care. It is even necessary to select another person to fill the position in which you would like to work when he's superior to you. You will still be an integral part.

People who borrow money create weak children. Their goal of making them stronger is lost as they seek to provide them with education through loans. They must be certain that they'll repay the loan and, for repayment, they must rely upon their kids. If not, it could be very risky. This is similar to purchasing a Lamborghini even if you don't have the money to buy Maruti Suzuki.

So, dropouts are frightened. They aren't afraid. Are you aware that this is the reason why Steve Jobs quit the company. In this article, I'll reveal the reasons Steve Jobs quit. He was actually the adopted kid. However, his mother was the one who demanded that the new parents accept a deal that would surely send him to university. In reality, the new parents were drop outs too. However, they were willing to sign the documents. In the following years, Steve Jobs's popularity grew and at the point the time came for him to enter college, He made a deal. The conditions were that he only went into Reed college. The college was expensive however it was his dream. His desires have changed the course of history numerous times. So why would he be able to fail in front of his parents. They signed off.

Then it became apparent that he was doing nothing that is new or exciting there. He only had an interest in the calligraphy course and he didn't even admit in to a class, even though he was officially. He began to doubt that he's ruined the father's fortune at the institution.

www.ingramcontent.com/pod-product-compliance
Lightning Source LLC
Chambersburg PA
CBHW071440080526
44587CB00014B/1928